N

I

MI

TEXT AND PERFORMANCE

General Editor: Michael Scott

The series is designed to introduce students to the themes, continuing vitality and performance of major dramatic works. The attention given to production aspects is an element of special importance, responding to the invigoration given to literary study by the work of leading contemporary critics.

The prime aim is to present each play as a vital experience in the mind of the reader – achieved by analysis of the text in relation to its themes and theatricality. Emphasis is accordingly placed on the relevance of the work to the modern reader and the world of today. At the same time, traditional views are presented and appraised, forming the basis from which a creative response to the text can develop.

In each volume, Part One: *Text* discusses certain key themes or problems, the reader being encouraged to gain a stronger perception both of the inherent character of the work and also of variations in interpreting it. Part Two: *Performance* examines the ways in which these themes or problems have been handled in modern productions, and the approaches and techniques employed to enhance the play's accessibility to modern audiences.

A synopsis of the play is given and an outline of its major sources, and a concluding Reading List offers guidance to the student's independent study of the work.

PUBLISHED

The Duchess of Malfi and The White Devil	Richard Cave
Hamlet	Peter Davison
The Winter's Tale	R. P. Draper
Death of a Salesman and The Crucible	Bernard Dukore
Tamberlaine and Edward II	George Geckle
Volpone	A. P. Hinchliffe
The Tempest	David L. Hirst
The Birthday Party and The Caretaker	Ronald Knowles
Measure for Measure	Graham Nicholls
The Merchant of Venice	Bill Overton
Richard II	Malcolm Page
Twelfth Night	Lois Potter
King Lear	Gámini Salgádo
Antony and Cleopatra	Michael Scott
Doctor Faustus	William Tydeman
Murder in the Cathedral and	
The Cocktail Party	William Tydeman
A Midsummer Night's Dream	Roger Warren
Henry the Fourth Parts 1 and 2	T. F. Wharton
Macbeth	Gordon Williams
Othello	Martin L. Wine

IN PREPARATION

Peer Gynt and Ghosts	Asbjorn Aarseth
The Real Thing	Robert Gordon
Much Ado About Nothing	Pamela Mason
Romeo and Juliet	Michael Scott
Waiting for Godot and	
Happy Days	Katherine Worth

DEATH OF A SALESMAN and THE CRUCIBLE

Text and Performance

BERNARD F. DUKORE

HUMANITIES PRESS INTERNATIONAL, INC.
Atlantic Highlands, NJ

© 1989 by Bernard F. Dukore

First published in 1989 in the United States of America by
Humanities Press International, Inc., Atlantic Highlands, NJ

Library of Congress Cataloging-in-Publication Data
Dukore, Bernard Frank, 1931–
Death of a salesman and The crucible/Bernard F. Dukore.
    p.   cm.—(Text and performance)
Bibliography: p.
Includes index.
ISBN 0–391–03572–X (pbk.): $8.50
1. Miller, Arthur, 1915–   Death of a salesman.   2. Miller,
Arthur, 1915–   Crucible.   3. Miller, Arthur, 1915–   Dramatic
production.   4. Salem (Mass.) in literature.   5. Witchcraft in
literature.   I. Title.   II. Series.
PS3525.I5156D434   1989
812′.52—dc19   88–2238
                                                   CIP

Printed in Hong Kong

CONTENTS

ACKNOWLEDGEMENTS

Quotations of the text of the plays are from Arthur Miller, *Collected Plays* (New York, Viking Press, 1960). Additional information on quotations, paraphrases and background are in the Reading List.

For their help in making theatre reviews available to me I am grateful to the following institutions and their staffs: the Billy Rose Theater Collection of the New York Public Library at Lincoln Center, the British Theatre Association and the Newspaper Library of the British Library at Colindale. The background information on China provided by Elizabeth Wichmann and Liu Dan has been very helpful. I also wish to thank Barbara, who was there at the start and present at the conclusion; her assistance has been major.

GENERAL EDITOR'S PREFACE

For many years a mutual suspicion existed between the theatre director and the literary critic of drama. Although in the first half of the century there were important exceptions, such was the rule. A radical change of attitude, however, has taken place over the last thirty years. Critics and directors now increasingly recognize the significance of each other's work and acknowledge their growing awareness of interdependence. Both interpret the same text, but do so according to their different situations and functions. Without the director, the designer and the actor, a play's existence is only partial. They revitalize the text with action, enabling the drama to live fully at each performance. The academic critic investigates the script to elucidate its textual problems, understand its conventions and discover how it operates. He may also propose his view of the work expounding what he considers to be its significance.

Dramatic texts belong therefore to theatre and to literature. The aim of the "Text and Performance" series is to achieve a fuller recognition of how both enhance our enjoyment of the play. Each volume follows the same basic pattern. Part One provides a critical introduction to the plays under discussion, using the techniques and criteria of the literary critic in examining the manner in which the work operates through language, imagery and action. Part Two takes the inquiry further into the plays' theatricality by focusing on selected productions of recent times so as to illustrate points of contrast and comparison in the interpretation of different directors and actors, and to demonstrate how the plays have worked on the modern stage. In this way the series seeks to provide a lively and informative introduction to major plays in their text and performance.

MICHAEL SCOTT

PART ONE: TEXT

1 INTRODUCTION

As I type these words, Arthur Miller's *Death of a Salesman* (1949) and *The Crucible* (1953) approach their 40th birthdays. Frequently reprinted, they are also frequently revived in the theatres of many countries. Miller's position as one of America's major dramatists is secure. Nineteen years after *The Crucible*'s first performance, Martin Gottfried labelled it 'powerful and heroic' (*Women's Wear Daily*, 1 May 1972). These qualities, by no means usual among modern dramatists, are less common among modern American dramatists, most of whom, as John Mason Brown says, make a fetish of understatement. 'They seem ashamed of the big things, embarrassed by the raw emotions, afraid of the naked passions, and unaware of life's brutalities and tolls.' The willingness and ability 'to strike unflinchingly upon the anvil of human sorrow is . . . the source of Arthur Miller's unique strength' (in Weales, *Salesman*).

Large subjects, elemental anguish, steadfast blows – throughout most of his work, Miller attempts to draw grand designs, not paint miniatures. Explicitly aiming to create the universal from the particular, he recognises that neither exists in isolation from the other. While he does not regard seriously plays of individual psychology despite the insight and precise observation they may contain, he simultaneously rejects drama that ignores or minimises psychology. Neither a polemicist nor an ideologue, he maintains that society is inside man and man inside society, or in a frequently quoted statement, 'The fish is in the water and the water is in the fish' ('The Shadows of the Gods').

The plays that are the subject of this book aspire to tragedy. Their protagonists are ordinary men, each with a kind of heroism, each intent on asserting, gaining and maintaining his identity, his 'name' as Miller often puts it. In his 'name' lies his stature as a human being, for it involves a sense of self often at odds with an indifferent or antagonistic society. Raymond Williams identifies the heart of Miller's dramatic pattern as 'tragedy – the loss of meaning in life turns to the struggle for meaning by death'. Although this loss is personal, 'it is always set in the context of a loss of social meaning, a loss of meaning in relationships' (in Corrigan, *Miller*).

Miller writes not of mythological figures but of his own countrymen, whose personal and social loss of meaning relates to disappointment in an American dream. *Death of a Salesman* presents a variety of American dreams; to his misfortune, the protagonist identifies himself with one. In *The Crucible*, the Puritans have subverted the American dream that brought them to New England; the consequence is an American nightmare.

These plays connect society not only to the individual but also to the family, that is, the larger society to the smaller social unit. In *Death of a Salesman* and *The Crucible*, the family crisis parallels the protagonist's societal crisis, and the larger society destroys the titular head of the smaller. Societal and familial betrayals are common to both plays. Both turn on adultery, which corrodes the relationship between husband and wife in *The Crucible*, between father and son in *Death of a Salesman*, but which neither play isolates as a sexual or psychological factor.

DEATH OF A SALESMAN

When *Death of a Salesman* first opened, reviewers were quick to observe its dramatic antecedents, notably Elmer Rice's *The Adding Machine*, which dramatises the alienated white-collar worker who is victim of a deadly conformist, materialistic society he does not comprehend; Clifford Odets's *Awake and Sing!*, which also contains a member of an older generation committing suicide so that a boy may inherit insurance money;

and Eugene O'Neill's *The Iceman Cometh*, whose chief figure, also a salesman, is a victim of pipe dreams. Scratch both Miller and O'Neill, and one finds Ibsen – in this case, *The Wild Duck*, another drama about illusions that inform one's life. Part of a cultural tradition embracing the mainstream of modern drama, *Death of a Salesman* has affinities that include German and American expressionism, whose techniques Miller consciously employs.

In Willy Loman, the alienated conformist man, Miller created what critics and audiences immediately recognised as a type, who thereby achieved mythic status. Willy's universal qualities do not eradicate his individual, psychological traits but, in harmony with Miller's dictum, interrelate with them. While Willy is not average, since he commits suicide, Miller notes, he embodies some of the more terrifying and destructive conflicts endemic in America – if not the world. A salesman 'represents optimism and illusion on one side, the bitter taste of failure on the other' (Michael Billington, *Guardian*, 6 April 1984); he embodies 'the contradictions of modern life: idealism and corruption, sincerity and falsehood, individualism and conformity' (Jack Kroll, *Newsweek*, 9 April 1984).

Miller's choice of names enhances his principal character's universality. Loman is indeed a low-man or common man. Cognominally as well as dramatically, he contrasts with the successful Dave Singleman, whose singularity makes him, as Willy fails to perceive, nonrepresentative. Loman's given name is also apt, for his defeats follow determined efforts to succeed. Linda's name suggests her beautiful soul, and Happy's a satisfaction with the system of which he like his father is a part. After fighting within himself, Biff overcomes the worse part of his nature and heritage to reject the system. But Biff and Happy are nicknames, apparently assigned because of the characters' nature: although we are not told Biff's real name, Happy says his own is Harold, and there is no reason not to believe him.

2 LANGUAGE

A common adverse criticism is that the play's language, which is deficient as poetry, makes it fall short of great drama. Labelling his review 'Poetry without Words', T. C. Worsley declared that nonverbal qualities do not constitute 'an adequate substitute for the words which just aren't there' (*New Statesman and Nation*, 6 Aug. 1949). Eric Bentley called its poetic passages 'bad poetry, the kind that sounds big and sad and soul-searching when heard for the first time and spoken very quickly within a situation that has already generated a good deal of emotion' but which is actually 'ham. Mere rhetorical phrasing' (in Hurrell). Joseph Wood Krutch said its language was 'as unmemorable, and as unquotable' as it was unpoetic (*Nation*, 5 March 1949), but such phrases as 'He's liked, but he's not – well liked', 'attention must be paid', and 'riding on a smile and a shoestring' have passed into the language, even finding their way into *Bartlett's Familiar Quotations*. Nowadays, critics usually applaud Miller's achievement. As Robert Cushman states (*Observer*, 23 Sept. 1979):

> The language of the play has been grievously underrated. Line after line flashes out. If Willy's dream of his funeral – 'all the old-timers with the strange license plates' – obviously strains for poetry, it just as obviously achieves it. And even the supposed clinkers have their validity. Why shouldn't Linda tell us 'attention must be paid to such a person'? Greek choruses make equally explicit appeals to our concern.

Names of products (Hastings refrigerator, Studebaker automobile), locales (Slattery's, Ebbets Field) and cities (Waterford, Boston) combine with period slang ('shoot some casino', 'dast blame this man') to achieve a cumulative effect that recalls Walt Whitman. Biff's 'You fake! You phony little fake! You fake!' is a triple-barrelled echo of 'I know he's a fake'. The title announces the protagonist's death, which language keeps in mind. Willy says that the builders have massacred the neighbourhood, Biff asks whether he knocked them dead and he replies that he slaughtered them. 'I'm tired to the death', says Willy soon after the play begins; shortly after the start of Act II, 'I slept like a dead one'. Miller's imagery is vivid and pungent: the lament of an ageing parent, 'Work a lifetime to pay off a house. You finally own it, and there's nobody to live in it'; the plea of an ordinary man's wife, 'he's only a little boat looking for a harbour'; the destruction of small city neighbourhoods by tall apartment buildings, 'Gotta break your neck to see a star in this yard'; planned obsolescence, 'I'm always in a race with the junkyard!' Willy's statements that the woods are burning variously evoke a preurbanised world, a sort of golden age in which he thinks he spent his childhood, and a jungle he believes his brother conquered. But as the play's recurrent imagery conditions us to recognise, various types of woods are afire. Because he was sacked, he tells his sons, the woods are burning. In the Boston hotel room, the Woman wonders if Biff's knocking at the door might signal a fire in the hotel.

3   What Happened When

Although today's readers do not require a glossary for *Death of a Salesman*, as they do for *The Merry Wives of Windsor*, young readers and spectators understand some of its specific references only by context, inference or specialised knowledge: Gene Tunney was a prizefighting champion, Jack Benny had a popular radio show, Spalding manufactured and sold sporting goods and all high school students in New York State were required to take examinations prepared by the State Board of Regents. More important are period assumptions that contribute to our understanding of character. Was Willy always unable to face reality? Does his statement in the remembered past that shops were closed for inventory constitute an excuse for his failure? Possibly because Willy tells Linda he imagined driving a red Chevrolet he had bought in 1928, some critics tend to think that his first hallucination about the past is set in that year, which precedes the Depression, for in it he talks to his offstage sons about cleaning this car. Yet in this scene Biff (34 in the dramatic present, he was born in 1915, the same year as Miller) is quite a ladies' man, is captain of his high school football team and must pass mathematics to be graduated and enter the University of Virginia in the Fall. Although the first attribute might be true of a thirteen-year-old, the others are not. More likely, Biff was then the age Bernard says he was when he was a high school senior, seventeen, which places all scenes of the past in 1932, when America was in the midst of the Depression and Franklin D. Roosevelt not yet elected President (or even nominated: the football game is in winter, the Regents Exam in spring). In 1932, about fifteen million were unemployed, many factories had either closed or were operating at low capacities and numerous shops were out of business, empty of customers or partly closed for inventory (having stocked too much merchandise). Thus, Willy's excuse for not having sold as much as he had hoped to, that three Boston stores were half closed for inventory, would be legitimate rather than a personal deficiency. Society, not he, had broken down. In 1932, Willy was not the only person to say that unless business picks up he does not know what he will do.

Other statements gain credibility when one recognises the period. Fewer cars were on the road in 1932 than today. During the Depression, pleasure driving was limited to the few who could afford it. Willy's boast that he could park his car in any New England street, where the police would protect it as if it were their own, is merely an exaggeration. His route was set and he was a 'regular'. With out-of-state license plates, the police might notice if anyone were to tamper with his car.

Whereas Willy says he has been with the Wagner firm for 34 years, Linda says March will mark his 36th anniversary. Since Biff is 34, Linda is probably correct for, in a psychologically apt touch, Miller has Willy confuse his time with the firm with his older son's age. Failure in one area mirrors failure in another, and personal meets professional in the Boston hotel scene. The approach of 36 years with the firm, moreover, places the year Willy joined it as 1913, prior to World War I, when America was smaller and more stable – a time when Dave Singleman might have done what Willy claims he did.

According to Linda, Willy is 63, which makes 1886 the year

he was born. Then, only 38 states were in the Union (10 less than when Miller wrote the play, a dozen less than today). Not until 1886 did Geronimo, the Apache Indian chief, surrender and not until 1890, the year Willy's father deserted his family, was the Battle of Wounded Knee fought – the last important clash between Indians and American soldiers, five years before the closing of the frontier. Whether Grandfather Loman went to Alaska to pan for gold (the gold rush did not begin there until 1896) or whether this was simply the reason the mother told the child is unimportant. What matters is that Willy's memory, through Ben's words, of their father driving a wagon across the Western states gains in credibility; and the background of the Brooklyn Loman thereby becomes a part of American legend. With Willy 63 in 1949, the Woman in Boston, who a stage direction tells us is not only proper looking but also the same age as Willy, is 46 in 1932, which means that she is not a young bimbo. Miller can be specific when he wishes to be specific.

By the same token, he is vague when he intends to be vague. As Willy's memory has it, Ben left home – a wagon in South Dakota (which Willy first recalls as Nebraska) – to search for their father in Alaska. Since Willy was a child, the reliability of his memory is questionable. The only specific pieces of information Miller provides are that Ben left at age seventeen, that when Willy imagines seeing him he is in his sixties – Willy's age in 1949 (probably so that Willy's older brother would not seem younger than him) – and that in 1936 or 1937, to pay for a radio correspondence course for Biff (vocational training for the son who failed to obtain a high school diploma), Willy pawned a diamond watch fob given him by Ben as a gift. In past and in present, Willy tries to give Biff a start in life.

After 1932, when Biff expected to be graduated from high school, he says he spent six or seven years working in New York City until Willy threw him out of the house. According to Happy, he stole basketballs almost ten years earlier. According to Willy, he left home over ten years before. Given the imprecision of memory, the statements do not essentially conflict: Biff left New York in 1938 or 1939. Biff also says that since leaving home before the war (for America, 7 Dec. 1941), he had twenty or thirty different types of jobs. Although he mentions herding cattle and being a farmhand, he says nothing about the military. What is clear is that Miller avoids the subject of World War II as much as he can. But as a realistic dramatist, he cannot ignore it completely. Three references, all in the restaurant scene, conjure it: Stanley, the waiter, wishes he had been drafted; Happy reminds Stanley of a champagne recipe he had brought back from overseas and just before Miss Forsythe enters, Happy relies on his built-in radar to announce that 'Strudel' is coming, a hint that he served in Germany or Austria. The point is not that one can discover references to World War II but that Miller takes pains to avoid stressing it. Just as he does not specifically name the Depression or Herbert Hoover, he does not mention Pearl Harbour or Hiroshima. To cite the Wall Street crash might turn *Death of a Salesman* into a social protest play. To name Adolf Hitler might make it a drama of alienated young men in the postwar era. Instead, by minimising the specific, Miller abstracts, therefore universalises, the drama. While a realistic past inheres in present dramatic action, the playwright stresses the latter, which contains enough concrete details to give the former credibility. Despite its realistic trappings, *Death of a Salesman* is universal, thus a more vivid dramatisation of a modern Everyman.

4   AMERICAN DREAMS, AMERICA, AMERICANS

In Miller's *A View from the Bridge*, the illegal immigrant Rodolpho explains that he did not come to America because of her tall buildings, electric lights, or automobiles, all of which Italy has. 'I want to be an American so I can work, that is the only wonder here – work.' To large numbers of immigrants, the American dream was the opportunity to find work at decent wages. To some, as to native Americans, it was the possibility of amassing a fortune, of progressing 'from rags to riches', a phrase popularised by the nineteenth-century American author Horatio Alger. The term 'cult of personality' was coined by Soviet Premier Nikita Khrushchev to derogate his predecessor, Joseph Stalin, but one might employ it to characterise an ideal of Americans, who use it flatteringly. As Walt Whitman asserted (*Democratic Vistas*, 1871): 'It is native personality, and that alone, that endows a man to stand before presidents or generals, or in any distinguish'd collection, with *aplomb* – and *not* culture, or any knowledge or intellect whatever'.

Willy Loman subscribes to this view and has taught his sons to believe not only in a success oriented society but also in the notion that native personality is the key to success therein. Insofar as the idea has some validity in Willy's profession, he is partly correct. Unfortunately, he goes further. The person who makes a good appearance, who creates personal interest in himself and who is well liked, he tells his sons, will get ahead in the business world. Charley's insight that no one liked J. P. Morgan except when he wore his pockets is lost on Willy.

With personality so important, the product (what a salesman sells) is less important. Although *Death of a Salesman* does not reveal what Willy sells, Miller in his own person does: 'Himself' (Introduction to *Collected Plays*). Willy is a commodity – which makes him more of an Everyman figure in today's world, where workers are commodities who are discarded when they can no longer function effectively. Buttressing the equation of Salesman and Everyman, Miller makes the Lomans three generations of salesmen. Willy claims his father sold flutes. The Lomans delude themselves that Biff was a salesman for Bill Oliver. In the restaurant, Happy presents himself as a salesman, offering Miss Forsythe a bottle of champagne that he claims is his brand.

To Willy the salesman, catchphrases and slogans become yardsticks: Waterford is famous for its clock, Boston as the cradle of the American revolution. The best products are measured by fame: his refrigerator has the largest ads (but it constantly breaks down) and his automobile has a well-known name (but it consumes fan belts maniacally). The inadequacies of what he buys mirror the inadequacies in his sales, which in turn reflect his inadequacies as a parent. His belief in the value of his occupation has the fanaticism that perhaps only a failure can have. Ironically, his failure to live profitably by false values helps provide him with stature as a man and sympathy as a character. As Miller states, such questions as gadget-infested comfort as a worthy ideal, an appropriate goal in the material world, fulfilment and an identity, and spiritual satisfaction in a materialistic society inform *Death of a Salesman*. Refusing to provide answers or to suggest alternatives that do not have limitations, he invites the audience to search for them. Unless one finds worthy values, he implies, the results can be catastrophic.

This American dream, chiefly embodied in Willy, is one of several presented in the play. Ben exemplifies another, the ruthless baron of industry, who succeeds by following the law of the jungle. As he reiterates, he entered the jungle at age seventeen and emerged at twenty-one when, by God, he was rich – though Miller dramatises the fact that God had nothing to do with his success: he gets the better of a seventeen-year-old boy, whose life he places at his mercy, by not fighting fairly with him (Biff lies on the ground, the point of Ben's umbrella poised above one of his eyes).

Willy tries to instill this ideal, together with his ideal of being well liked, which he finds compatible, in his sons. As football hero, Biff succeeds, towering above his classmates, defeating the rival team. What Willy does not realise is that probably the only circumstance wherein one can succeed as an extraordinary person and still be well liked is athletics in high school.

Biff's success on the football field hints at another American dream, which Bernard fulfills: industrious efforts bring success. If Willy had the wrong dreams, right dreams were available to him. Biff worked as hard and successfully at football as Bernard does at academic studies. Major universities want him not because of who he knows and his smile, but because of demonstrated abilities. Furthermore, for all Willy's jargon about contacts and personality, he works ten to twelve hours daily.

Another American dream is that of the family as bedrock of society: whatever Willy's deficiencies as breadwinner and personal charmer, his wife adores him and until Biff's discovery of his adultery, he and Happy idolise him. Another dream is that of the farmhand and cowboy; Biff, who finds this emotionally fulfilling, tries to endow it with transcendant qualities. Still another is that of personal satisfaction by building something with one's own hands; Willy, as Biff perceives, does not fully comprehend its real value to him. 'He had the wrong dreams', says Biff. 'All, all wrong.' But Biff is not Miller's *raisonneur*. The Miller character with *all* the wrong dreams is the neurotic protagonist of *A View from the Bridge*, who unlike Willy does not have a satisfactory sexual relationship with his wife, causes the arrest of relatives and wants to prevent his stepchild from getting a job.

While *Death of a Salesman* condemns a social system control-led by wealth, oriented towards the acquisition of money, and indifferent to human beings, this theme is only part of the picture. 'Only the most fatuous observer could think of *Death of a Salesman* as a propaganda play, and yet it manages to go deeply enough into contemporary values to be valid and frightening social criticism' (Richard Watts, Jr, *New York Post*, 11 Feb. 1949). Social criticism notwithstanding, it dramatises 'a man's destruction through the tearing-away of his protective covering of lies and self-deceit' (Peter Jenkins, *Spectator*, 29 Sept. 1979). Reminding readers of the original title, *The Inside of His Head*, Ruby Cohn calls Miller's achievement 'the skillful dramatisation of Willy's last hours to reveal what goes on inside his head' (in Martin).

To some, the play's fusion of the social and psychological is a dramatic weakness. They point to Willy's personal faults, the capitalist Charley's virtues as a friend and approval of Bernard's success in a capitalist world as marks of fuzzy thinking: the acceptance of middle-class values while condem-ning them. In the Communist paper *The Daily Worker* (14 Feb. 1949), Lee Newton asserts, 'Ambiguity is not the result of clear thematic thinking'. In *Partisan Review* (June 1949), Eleanor Clark condemns Miller for avoiding responsibility for his ideas: after Howard fires Willy, which demonstrates that 'the capitalist system . . . has done Willy in', Miller 'withdraws behind an air of pseudo-universality, and hurries to present some cruelty or misfortune due either to Willy's own weakness, as when he refuses his friend's offer of a job . . . or gratuitously from some other source, as in the quite unbelievable scene of the two sons walking out on their father in the restaurant', thus creating 'an intellectual muddle' (in Weales, *Salesman*). Miller claims to attempt a synthesis of social and psychological, says Eric Bentley, who finds only thesis and antithesis. 'In fact, I never know what a Miller play is about: politics or sex. If *Death of a Salesman* is political, the key scene is the one with the tape recorder; if it is sexual, the key scene is the one in the Boston hotel' (*New Republic*, 19 Dec. 1955).

Others praise Miller for that very synthesis. According to Ronald Hayman, 'Miller uses sex as a means of carrying his social argument forward'. To Benjamin Nelson, 'One of the strengths of *Death of a Salesman* is its refusal to pin blame exclusively on a person, an institution, or even on an entire society'. Actually, Miller agrees with the 'clear-eyed' view that 'When a man gets old you fire him, you have to, he can't do the work' and celebrates this 'common sense of businessmen, who love the personality that wins the day but know that you've got to have the right goods at the right time' (Introduction to *Collected Plays*). 'I've always tried to think otherwise', says Willy, whose view that personality matters more than the ability to deliver the goods is childish. Thus, young Howard several times calls him 'kid', as does young Bernard. Yet despite Miller's own view of the matter, and despite Willy's immaturity, Howard's rejection of him is dramatised as callous and brutal. One of the pernicious, or at least ironic, features of capitalism is that in dealing with subordinates capitalists do not always act as capitalists. Old man Wagner showed off his baby to his employees, whom he may have asked what they thought of the name Howard. Was business only business to Father Wagner? Of course, but the businessman uses the ethos of family to bind employees. Howard greets Willy not as an employee but as a member of his family, urging him to listen to the voices of daughter, son and wife. But when the employee invokes the personal in his own behalf, the employer rejects it because business is not family: it is, tautologically, business, and in it everyone must pull his own weight. Underscoring Howard's insensitivity, two unintentional *coups de grace* follow his sacking of Willy. First, he tells Willy to pull himself together and to take as long as five minutes to do so since he needs the office. Next, he asks Willy to return the sample merchandise 'whenever you can this week', which may be an oxymoron.

To use Miller's formulation, the fish is in the sea and the sea in the fish. *Death of a Salesman* is neither a social tract nor a psychological treatise. As Harold Clurman says, its point is 'not that our economic system does not work, but that its ideology distorts man's true nature' (*New Republic*, 28 Feb. 1949). The father contends with the salesman, the values of family with those of business, love with financial success. But does not the desire for love inhere in Willy's occupation, and does not the hope of financial success link to the family? Does the salesman kill the father when monetary values dominate (the inheritance for Biff, buying his love, as it were)? Perhaps, but the values of the father have succeeded (remarkably, his son loves him).

5   CHARACTERS

Willy   Each week, Willy is on the road for five days. With more than 70 per cent of his time away from his family, he focuses on his work and the values associated with it, but his infidelities disturb him profoundly (Linda seems unaware of them). Characters he remembers personify his aims. Like Ben, he wants to succeed in business, Like his father, who made flutes, he makes things with his hands, and he brags to Charley of the ceiling he put up. Like the legendary Dave Singleman, he wants to be well liked. To be well liked, he tries like the stereotypical salesman of popular mythology to amuse people with risqué jokes. In the remembered past, he slaps the Woman in Boston's fanny and exclaims, 'bottoms up!' In time present, he asks Charley's secretary, 'How're ya? Workin'? Or still honest?'

A failure in his work, he fears the present and romanticises the past, to which his mind continually reverts. But he fears the past as well – which may be why he romanticises it.

Whereas at the start of the play he recalls a happy time on the road, at the end he recalls a traumatic experience there. Alienated from his beloved older son, he is also alienated from the world around him and from his past. His first appearance is an image of alienation: a solitary figure, dwarfed by his surroundings, weighed down by his actual and emotional luggage. Setting the tone of the play, this initial view defines Willy negatively, not by what he did but by what he did not do. His statement that nothing happened to make him return prematurely from his sales trip means he was not in an auto accident. The nothing that happened was an inability to drive beyond a northern suburb of New York City.

His daydreams while driving were occasioned by the beautiful scenery he passed − a striking contrast to the ugly apartment buildings surrounding his house. Such contrast or contradiction is a frequent characterising device. Although Willy claims identity as the firm's New England man, he complains that he is not in the New York office. He says the Chevrolet is the greatest car ever made but repairs are so expensive its manufacture should be prohibited. After he twice condemns Biff for laziness, he admiringly says the boy is not lazy. Exclaiming that Biff's not finding himself at age 34 is disgraceful, he soon announces that some eminent men do not get started until later in life. He calls himself well liked but admits that people do not take to him. He first declares that a man should have few words, next that since life is short some jokes are in order, then that he jokes too much. His speech reflects his conflicting values and lack of control. When a complaint about the encroaching apartment buildings is succeeded by one about his salesmanship ('Population is getting out of control. The competition is maddening!'), he reveals the latter to be his real fear − ironic, since a salesman should welcome many potential customers.

One ought not to accept Willy's statements at face value. Whether he recalls his father (whom he last saw when he was four), Ben (whom be barely knew) or Dave Singleman, we cannot accept his say-so or (with Ben) the projection of his think-so. He so frequently distorts reality, we can be sure that he does not fully comprehend himself or society. From a statement that Father Wagner asked him what he thought of the name Howard for his son, he leaps to 'I named him Howard'. His counsel to Biff on how to conduct himself in a business interview reverberates on himself. He advises Biff to be serious, not to say boy's words like 'Gee', be modest or look worried. Instead, he should begin with a few jokes, for personality will win the day. 'And if anything falls off the desk while you're talking to him – like a package or something – don't you pick it up. They have office boys for that.' The contradiction between advice to be serious and to tell jokes alerts us to notice that Willy does not follow his own guidance. His final speech in Act I starts 'Gee', which he repeats soon after Act II begins and uses again when he enters the restaurant. When he sees his employer, Willy is worried and modest, if not subservient. At one point, Howard *'looks for his lighter. Willy has picked it up and gives it to him.'*

Miller's portrait of Willy Loman is more subtle than one may first realise. He wants his sons to succeed more spectacularly than anyone else and is ashamed that they have not done so. Upon learning of the adult Bernard's success, Willy is *'shocked, pained'*, but also *'happy'*. To ask Bernard, whom he had despised as puny, the secret of his success and Biff's failure requires a great effort; but Willy makes the effort. Although he loves his wife, he subconsciously blames her for his failure. If he had gone to Alaska with Ben when he had the chance to do so, he laments, his life would have been different. Apart from the dubiousness of whether a tycoon would have said to Willy, at 46 and with no experience of managing a business, 'I need a man to look after things for me. . . . Screw on your fists and you can fight for a fortune up there', Willy's hallucination has Linda *'frightened of Ben and angry at him'*, arguing that Willy has a good job, is well liked and will some day be made a member of the firm. Furthermore, as John Elsom observes (*Listener*, 27 Sept. 1979): 'We do not learn about Loman's dilemmas through Loman's eyes, because we always know more about his failure than he does'. An 'object lesson', Willy 'is not discovering hard realities on our behalf'. In contrast to *A View from the Bridge*, no *raisonneur* tells us about him.

Miller calls Willy a true believer, a zealot. If he did not have 'a very profound sense that his life as lived had left him hollow, he would have died very contentedly polishing his car on some Sunday morning at a ripe old age'. Because he cannot realise the ideals to which he is intensely dedicated, he feels frantic. He seeks 'a kind of ecstasy in life which the machine civilisation deprives people of. He is looking for his selfhood, for his immortal soul, so to speak' ('Morality and Modern Drama').

As Neil Carson points out, Willy is a son as well as a father. Insecure from childhood, when his father abandoned the family, he has always felt 'kind of temporary' about himself. Thus, he is overly supportive of his older son. When Biff fails math, Willy blames the teacher. Thus too, he excessively adores the boy. 'If young Biff steals it is courage. If he captains a football team, the world is watching' (William Hawkins, *New York World-Telegram*, 11 Feb. 1949). In emulating Dave Singleman by choosing his profession, Willy hopes to gain what Singleman possesses, love, which is what he demands from his son. Beyond the contrast to urbanisation, the garden suggests that Willy's seeds cannot take root or develop. Failing with garden and sons, Willy in the final act tries to plant seeds at night using a flashlight – an image that combines family, home and society.

Biff and Happy   Among the play's polarities are the family and the jungle, domestic security and the dangerous world of business. Willy's father and brother chose the latter, and while Ben had a wife and seven sons, his primary identification is with business, which he calls a jungle. Willy is drawn to both poles. Devoted to his family, he regards society as a jungle with burning woods, predatory animals and competitors trying to beat him to the spoils. Neither of his sons marries or fosters a family – that is, neither emulates him. Biff's actions parody adventurousness and business enterprise: punching cattle and petty theft. Replacing marriage with one-night stands, Happy like Willy does not leave home.

Despite Biff's rejection of his father after their encounter in Boston, Willy's ways are imprinted in him. In the restaurant, he mimics his father's line of patter. When Letta asks whether he was ever on a jury, he quips, 'No, but I been in front of them'. The hotel scene, says Carson, gives him a shock of sufficient force that he cannot perceive the truth about himself for seventeen years. 'His anger with his father serves as an excuse to avoid looking for the real causes of his failure which are in himself.' As if to demonstrate the worthlessness of his father's real values (as he discovered them in Boston), Biff carries one such value to an extreme: encouraged to 'get away with' thievery when a boy (stealing lumber), he continues stealing as an adult, as if to demonstrate how wrong his father was. Furthermore, Biff refuses to do what his father hopes he will do: complete his studies, attend a university and succeed at business. Yet he continues to seek parental approval as a man. He does not know what he wants but what he is supposed to want, and he becomes particularly dissatisfied with his life out West in the spring (the anniversary of his discovery of his father's adultery). Losing confidence in his father, he loses confidence in himself (with women as well as in business). Verbally connecting his father and himself, his plea 'help him' turns in the next breath to 'help me'. Whereas both have business interviews, only Biff gains self-knowledge as a result. His new recognition consists of embracing an aspect of Willy that Willy rejects as a worthwhile career goal: an uncompetitive life in the outdoors.

Biff's recognition that he and his father are 'a dime a dozen' conflicts with his father's insistence that each is a unique individual. Miller regrets that Biff's perception, designed to provide uplift, does not more adequately counterbalance Willy's disaster. Fortunately, he has not revised the play to strengthen it, since it might then become an italicised message. Willy's charge that Biff ruined his life because Biff blames him is accurate – as Biff inadvertently concedes: 'I never got anywhere because you blew me so full of hot air, I could never stand taking orders from anybody! That's whose fault it is!' To insist 'I'm nothing' is to deny Willy's hopes that he would be everything, and to urge Willy to admit the same is as vengeful as Willy claims. By saying 'There's no spite in it any more', Biff tacitly admits there once was.

Critics who complain that Biff's new vision diminishes horizons, is a joyless recognition of failure, and is vague, trite and romantic, miss the point. Through Biff, Miller presents a nonidealistic understanding that for people like him ideals bring frustration, failure and loss of self-esteem. While the myth of the last frontier may have diminished from Alaskan horizons to the New England territory to a ranch, the last brings greater satisfaction to Biff than urbanised drudgery.

Nevertheless, Biff's self-recognition conveys a sense of loss. However commendable Biff's preparedness to leave may be, Willy's commitment to his sons and his determination to hope and fight may be a more uplifting vision – despite its futility. The dichotomy provides tension and complexity.

On one level, Happy understands his father: a poor salesman, he is 'sometimes . . . a sweet personality'. On another, he fails to learn from his father's mistaken values. 'He fought it out here' echoes Willy's 'We'll do it here, Ben!' The younger, less-favoured son tries harder than the older to be like, therefore loved by, the father. He claims to want a girl just like the girl who married dear old dad – one who would resist a hustler like himself – but since he says, using a cliché as his father would, 'They broke the mould when they made her', he does not seek a woman with her qualities. Like his father, he bloats his professional achievements; and he condemns Biff because he cannot earn much money out West. Recycling his father's liked/well liked antithesis, he encourages Miss Forsythe to disengage herself for the evening: 'Don't try, honey, try hard'. Like his father's brags, his should not be accepted at face value. Would a man who built a magnificent estate on Long Island be a good friend of a person like Happy? Because the man lived in it for two months, then sold it to build another, Happy concludes, he cannot enjoy it once it has been finished; but his conclusion may reflect his incomprehension: the man may have built it to sell at a profit. Is Happy so influential that manufacturers offer him hundred dollar bribes (equal to about six hundred today) to throw business their way?

Like Willy, Happy is alienated. Despite a profusion of women (the pick-up we see makes that boast credible), he calls himself lonely. Unwilling to commit himself, he keeps 'knockin' them over and it doesn't mean anything'. While this statement anticipates Willy's, that the Woman in Boston means nothing, differences are more striking: Willy talks of one woman (the only affair we know of), he offers a humane explanation and his emotional commitment to Linda is real. Without a family to sustain him, Happy is a deterioration from his father. Like Willy, Happy wants to succeed at business. But his imagery debases religion to monetary terms: when the marketing manager enters the store 'the waves part in front of him' and unlike the spiritual aura exuded by Moses when he led the Israelites across the Red Sea, the aura surrounding the manager consists of 52 000 dollars a year.

Both Willy and Linda define Happy's status as less-favoured younger son. After Biff tells Willy of the football he 'borrowed':

> WILLY: (*laughing with him at the theft*) I want you to return that.
> HAPPY: I told you he wouldn't like it.
> BIFF: (*angrily*) Well, I'm bringing it back!
> WILLY: (*stopping the incipient argument, to Happy*) Sure, he's gotta practise with a regulation ball, doesn't he? (*To Biff*) Coach'll probably congratulate you on your initiative!

Willy sides with the older son against the younger. In time present, he and his wife do the same when Happy seeks their approbation and notice. In Act I, after Willy reiterates that Biff has greatness in him and Linda cries to her darling to sleep well, the ignored younger brother calls for approval: 'I'm gonna get married, Mom'. Her response: 'Go to sleep, dear'. His father's: 'Keep up the good work'. Although Linda demands attention for Willy, she gives none to Happy, whom Willy also ignores. In Act II, Happy puts his arm around his mother and addresses his father: 'I'm getting married, Pop, don't forget it. I'm changing everything. I'm gonna run that department before the year is up'. Willy turns away from him. Small wonder, then, that Happy fails to respond to Biff's charges that he does nothing for their father, who means nothing to him. The neglected son has his revenge. Ushering Miss Forsythe out of the restaurant, he interrupts her suggestion that he tell his father he is leaving: 'No, that's not my father. He's just a guy'. More basically, he revenges himself on his father and brother through philandering. By refusing to marry, he rejects his father's value system; to prove he is more of a man than his brother, an athletic hero, he excels in the sexual arena.

Linda   Willy calls Linda his foundation and support. She tries
to make the boys treat him decently and encourages him when
he needs reassurance. She is neither stupid nor overly passive,
as some assert. Were she to nag Willy to face reality, he might
emulate his father and abandon the family; and critics might
condemn her for the zealotry of Gregers Werle in *The Wild
Duck*. Not as deluded about reality as Willy is, she wonders
whether Bill Oliver will remember Biff; and she is far from a
doormat when her sons fail their duties to their father.

Miller most fully reveals Linda in three scenes from which
Willy is absent. In the first, she primarily pleads his case as a
man. Although he never earned much money or was the most
wonderful person in the world, he is a human being in crisis,
to whom attention should be paid. A small person can be as
exhausted as a great one, and while his business associates do
not accord him recognition, neither do his sons, for whose
benefit he worked. Perhaps the most famous speech in the
play, it defines Willy and gives him stature. In the second
scene, primarily pleading his case as a father, she castigates
her sons for having deserted him as they would not have a
stranger. In the third, she eulogises a husband she loves. Far
from demonstrating stupidity, her incomprehension of why he
committed suicide derives from what she, not the audience,
was aware of. When she last saw Willy, he was happy because
Biff loved him. These three scenes provide a more rounded
view of Willy and Linda than we might otherwise receive.

Other men   Willy's neighbour Charley is a capitalist successful
enough to give Willy 50 dollars a week for a long time and to
offer Willy a job. Charley contrasts with Willy in other key
respects. Unlike Willy, he is not possessed by an ideal. He
advises Willy to forget about Biff and not take his failure or
animosity too hard. 'That's easy enough for you to say', replies
Willy. The compassionate Charley retorts, 'That ain't easy
for me to say'. Not only is Charley an alternative to Howard,
thereby modifying what might be a simplistic attack on
businessmen, he is also an alternative to Willy as representative
of middle-class America. His tribute during the Requiem does
not make him a *raisonneur*, though he probably speaks in part

for the author. In context, his words stop an argument between Happy and Biff, to whom he tries to explain the sort of man Willy was.

Charley's successful son contrasts with Willy's unsuccessful sons. As Charley befriends Willy, Bernard befriends Biff. His advice to Willy resembles his father's: at times it is better for a man to walk away. He demonstrates his affection for Willy by attending his funeral – which Willy's employer does not do.

Like Willy, Howard Wagner is a doting father whose two children are two years apart. Like Willy, he is a product of a consumer society; and if Willy could afford to do so, he too would buy a wire recorder. While this businessman uses ties of family-like friendship in his own behalf, Howard prefers not to act like an ogre. He might have fired Willy before, and when he does so it is because Willy provides an excuse other than failure to sell the product: he loses his temper and yells at Howard. Before the play begins, Howard has reduced Willy to working solely on commission – an insult to an old employee and a move that requires no negative cash flow – which is not the mark of a decent man, only of one who does not go all the way in indecency. With Howard, Miller demonstrates that all successful businessmen are not as kind or decent as Charley.

More ruthless than Howard is Ben. An outright symbol of the merciless, self-made millionaire, he is seen exclusively from Willy's viewpoint.

Other women   In contrast to the wife and mother symbolised by Linda, Miss Forsythe and Letta represent the millions of single women available to men like Happy.

Despite the dreamlike quality of the scenes with the Woman in Boston (like Ben, seen solely from Willy's viewpoint), Miller reveals that she is as lonely as Willy. When he tries to hustle her out of the room she feels '*angry, humiliated*' – like a football kicked by insensitive players. Despite her brief appearances, Miller pays attention to her.

6   DRAMATIC STRUCTURE

As characters reflect each other, so do scenes and sequences, seamlessly interweaving. After Howard fires Willy from his job, the imaginary Ben offers him one, then the real Charley does. Following Willy's visit to his boss, Biff narrates his visit to a former boss – which like his father's ends disastrously. The sons' sexual encounter in the restaurant interconnects with their father's in a hotel room.

Whereas Act I begins with worry about death, dejection about a job and estrangement between Willy and Biff, it ends with hope and encouragement in all aspects. Act II starts with an exhilarated Willy holding great expectations for himself and his sons; it ends with his embrace of death. At the opening of Act I, Willy's desperation is reflected by the backyard, about which he is disconsolate since not even grass grows any more. His new optimism at the opening of Act II is reflected by his cheerful suggestion of buying a place in the country where he will raise vegetables. Early in Act I, when Willy hopes Biff will find himself, he optimistically says, 'I'll put my money on Biff' – which he does at the end of the play. Early in Act II, confident that Howard will transfer him to the New York office, Willy exclaims, 'I will never get behind a wheel the rest of my life!' – but he will, one last time.

Like Ibsen's compact prose dramas – indeed, like the well-made play against which Ibsen reacted – *Death of a Salesman* has as structural focus, a climax that revolves around a hidden secret. Although the scene in Howard's office is just as crucial to the play as the scene in Boston, the latter is its structural pivot, placed in the climactic spot, after the office scene and near the play's end, and artfully foreshadowed. Some reviewers castigate the scene as trite and simplistic; others defend it as psychologically valid. A serious criticism is Ruby Cohn's (in Martin): 'A phoney dream of success should be exploded by a scene about the phoniness of success, and not about illicit sex'. Perhaps a more fruitful line of inquiry would be to ask that since the hotel scene is clearly climactic, of what is it the climax? Because it reveals Willy's guilt and the effects of its discovery on Biff, the answer revolves around the nature of the relationship between father and son, which is the central theme. Far from being reductive, it implicates the others. Not only does Biff witness Willy's gift of the stockings promised to his mother (betrayal of the ideal of family), it makes him see the hollowness of his father's business values (the ideal of society), of which Willy held himself up as exemplar. In Willy's first memory of the past, he announces that if his sons become well liked, they will succeed – as he has, since he never needs to wait to see a buyer. In Boston, the Woman tells Willy that henceforth, thanks to her, he will not have to wait to see buyers. While Biff does not hear her, the entire experience connects to him; furthermore, Willy tells Biff three times that she is a buyer. Rejecting success in business, since it betrays his mother, he rejects his lying father and business itself. Particularly notable, the discovery of the secret is private, not public. As Brian Parker states, the play progresses towards 'the gradual admission by Willy *to himself* of his own guilt'; unlike discoveries in Ibsenite drama, Willy's guilt 'is never openly discussed between him and Biff, and Linda and Hap never learn of it at all: the sole importance is that Willy himself should recognise it' (in Corrigan, *Miller*).

A compact work, *Death of a Salesman* confines itself to the last 24 hours in its protagonist's life. Although the past continually intrudes upon the dramatic present, as in Ibsenite drama, Miller does not treat the past in terms of conventional exposition. Instead, as Willy remembers past events, his memories take place on stage. The play's time framework is complex. As Edward Murray perceives, Miller dramatises three types of time: objective time present (we see what occurs, as if in real life), subjective time past (enacted as Willy presently imagines the past) and a mixture of both. Take, for example, the four scenic units in the first part of Act I. The play begins with objective time present (Willy and Linda, Biff and Happy, Willy and Linda), continues with subjective time past (Willy imagines himself with his family in 1932), follows with objective time present (Willy, Happy, Charley), then a mixture of objective and subjective (Willy talks to Charley and his dead brother), and so forth. In the restaurant scene of Act II, Miller dazzlingly employs combinations of time in rapid sequence.

Often, critics call the scenes involving the past *flashbacks*;
but flashbacks are precisely what they are not. A cinematic
term, a flashback is a break in chronological sequence which
dramatises an event or exchange that occurred in the past.
Although one might embroider this definition to note that the
break may be subjective rather than objective, the former is
rarely the case (Alfred Hitchcock's *Stage Fright* and Akira
Kurosawa's *Rashomon* are virtually unique in this respect: in
flashbacks, characters lie about or distort what happened).
The usual flashback convention is that the dramatisation of
the past is reality.

Events in time present trigger not events in time past but
Willy's present view of such events. When Howard sacks him
his mind conjures Ben, who offers him a job. The first
dramatised scene of the past, not a flashback but a hallucination, depicts a time when Willy apparently enjoyed what he
now misses. Now, he complains of apartment houses crowding
his home; then, they had not been constructed and there were
trees whose branches might hit his roof. Now, he cannot get
past Yonkers and he is estranged from his older son; then, he
returns from New England a seeming success to boys who
adore him and emulate him (after Willy calls Charley liked
but not well liked, Biff says the same of Bernard). But the
supposedly safe retreat is filled with hidden perils. Biff might
fail math, therefore not be graduated; Biff steals; Willy's
earnings are lower than he initially boasts. In a dramatically
daring hallucination within the first hallucination, his infidelity
haunts him as the vision and laughter of the Woman in
Boston interrupt him. The hallucination farther from reality
comments not only on reality but also on the hallucination
closer to reality, and its dramatic technique is nonrealistic:
'Willy, Willy, are you going to get up, get up, get up, get up?'

Even Willy's most idealised view of the past, Ben, is a
criticism of himself. Salesmanship, says Ben, provides nothing
upon which to lay one's hands. With a single gadget, their
father could earn more money in a week than a person like
Willy could earn in a lifetime.

The merger of hallucination and objective reality is integral
to Miller's dramatic method. As Benjamin Nelson explains,
hallucination 'indicates the agonising intensity of the sales-

man's search for the meaning of his life' and 'by insolubly linking the final day of Willy's life with the years that have shaped this day, it gives his life and death a dramatic cohesiveness'.

The play ends not with the titular death but with a funeral – an ironic contrast to that of Dave Singleman. Each speaking for himself, no mourner explains what the play is about. Happy reaffirms Willy's dream. Charley talks of Willy's cheerful and confident appearance. Biff offers an alternative to his father's values. Linda speaks of her love and the irony that with the mortgage paid off, 'We're free'. The play makes us disinclined to accept either Happy's valuation or Charley's refusal to blame Willy, but it also makes us wary of accepting Biff's recognition that he and his father are ten cents per dozen as the final word for anyone but Biff himself (Willy's zest for life and full commitment may make him seem more valuable than that). While we understand more of Willy than Linda does, it is appropriate that the play's last words speak affectionately of the salesman. Despite its ambiguities, the Requiem offers an alternative to a bleak note struck amid utter incomprehension.

7   TRAGEDY?

From the outset, *Death of a Salesman* raised the question: Is it a tragedy? For the most part, reviewers answered affirmatively. The play has 'exaltation as well as tragic meaning' (Howard Barnes, *New York Herald Tribune*, 11 Feb. 1949). In Biff 'lies the catharsis of the play, the journey through "pity and fear" to a heightened sense of what the individual must mean to himself and to others. . . . This is not the whole answer. But it is more than Willy perceived' (John Beaufort, *Christian Science Monitor*, 19 Feb. 1949). Eric Bentley disagreed: the tragedy destroys the social drama, its catharsis reconciling or persuading us to disregard the material conditions against which the social drama protests, and the social drama destroys the tragedy, in that the subject of the little man as victim

arouses pity but no terror, for he is too passive to be a tragic
hero (in Hurrell).

While Michael Billington does not invoke Aeschylus's
Oresteia, he might do so when he argues that 'the weaknesses
of one generation are visited upon the next' (*Guardian*, 2 Sept.
1979). In two Loman generations, almost ritualistically, older
brothers leave the family and their names, Ben and Biff,
alliteratively hint at a connection; younger brothers remain,
Willy and Happy, whose names have a suffix that also hints
at a connection. Far-fetched? Not if one considers the friends,
alliteratively connected, Hamlet and Horatio, and the working
partners, connected by suffix, Claudius and Polonius.

Some examinations of modern tragedy derive from unexam-
ined assumptions. 'Where the causes of disaster . . . can be
resolved through technical or social means', says George
Steiner, 'we may have serious drama, but not tragedy. More
pliant divorce laws could not alter the fate of Agamemnon;
social psychiatry is no answer to *Oedipus*. But saner economic
relations or better plumbing *can* resolve some of the grave
crises in the dramas of Ibsen'. By contrast, 'Tragedy is
irreparable. It cannot lead to just and material compensation
for past suffering'. This passage raises more questions than it
answers. More pliant divorce laws might have opened other
possibilities to Clytemnestra than murder. Although neurotic
complexes are not even issues for Oedipus at Thebes,
Sophocles establishes a different view of responsibility and
law when an older Oedipus is at Colonus. Saner economic
relations would not resolve the most basic problems in *A Doll's
House*, and while better plumbing would alleviate the problems
in *An Enemy of the People*, few consider it a tragedy. Concerning
Death of a Salesman, if one begins a question with 'What if',
the apparent conflict between tragic and technical or social
might disappear. What if Howard agreed to Willy's request
to transfer to New York? One source of aggravation would be
alleviated, but not the elemental sources of Willy's discontent,
which lie in his relationship with his older son and the world
in which they live.

After dismissing Ibsen, Steiner admits, 'None of this, I
know, is a definition of tragedy'. Then: 'But any neat abstract
definition would mean nothing. When we say "tragic drama"

we know what we are talking about; not exactly, but well enough to recognise the real thing'. Do we? And who are 'we'? Is *The Bacchae*, which Steiner applauds, a tragedy? Does it contain recognition by the protagonist? Who, for that matter, is the protagonist? Usually, 'the real thing' consists of only a few exemplars, but the 'we' who recognise them exclude T. S. Eliot, who calls *Hamlet* 'most certainly an artistic failure' (*The Sacred Wood*). Furthermore, what of the social strictures that inform the *Iphigenia in Aulis* of Euripides? Does any vacillating warrior-hero in it have stature? What of the cowardly, selfish, mean-spirited central figures in his *Electra*? Does the protagonist of *Antigone* acquire self-knowledge? Is not that of *Prometheus Bound* a victim? As M. W. Steinberg rhetorically asks, are we reconciled to or uplifted by the deaths of Othello or Cordelia? Does Othello's weakness or flaw merit his death? (in Corrigan, *Miller*). The point of this paragraph is not to denigrate these plays but to demonstrate that many critics fail to question them as closely or along the same lines as they do *Death of a Salesman*.

Each age creates its own type of tragedy. In Shakespeare's day, a drama of revenge was a tragedy, whether *Spanish* or *Revenger's* or *Hamlet*. The anonymous contemporary author of *A Warning for Fair Women* knew what the audience meant by it. In the Induction, a character called Tragedy demands passionate emotions, tear-jerking and exaggeratedly rhetorical speech. Mocking him, a character called Comedy says that in tragedy a person kills a multitude for a crown, a chorus howls an omen, a ghost whines and someone cries for revenge – all amidst special effects, like smoke. According to Pierre Corneille, writing in seventeenth-century France, pity without terror sufficed for tragedy ('Second Discourse', in Dukore).

'I have often wished', Miller declares, 'that I had never written a word on the subject of tragedy' ('Author's Foreword'). No matter, the controversy would have occurred. '*In all* [Charley] *says, despite what he says, there is pity, and, now, trepidation.*' These terms, a short hop from 'pity and fear', put us in Aristotelian territory. We remain there when Biff twice calls Willy a prince and when he asks if Willy's rubber hose is designed to 'make a hero out of you? . . . There'll be no pity for you, you hear it?' To say that a hero and pity are just what Miller has in mind for Willy is not to disparage him. After all, Sophocles often has people call Oedipus great.

Miller establishes his basic ideas on tragedy in three essays: 'Tragedy and the Common Man', 'The Nature of Tragedy' and Introduction to *Collected Plays*. Insisting that the common man is as fit a tragic subject as a king, he denigrates any suggestion in Aristotle's *Poetics* that he might not be. Slaves, which existed in Aristotle's society, have no alternatives, thus cannot be heroes of any drama; but when people have alternatives that might change their lives, as they do today, then whatever their rank they are capable of tragic stature. Our notion of the tragic hero should change with the times. When Miller states that 'if the exaltation of tragic action were truly a property of the high-bred character alone, it is inconceivable that the mass of mankind should cherish tragedy above all other forms, let alone be capable of understanding it' and 'If rank or nobility of character was indispensable, then it would follow that the problems of those with rank were the particular problems of tragedy', he echoes such writers as George Lillo – tragedy 'is more truly august in proportion to . . . the numbers that are properly affected by it' (Dedication to *The London Merchant*, in Dukore) – and G. E. Lessing: 'The misfortunes of those whose circumstances most resemble our own must naturally penetrate most deeply into our hearts, and if we pity kings, we pity them as human beings, not as kings' (*Hamburg Dramaturgy*, in Dukore).

Many who adversely criticise *Death of a Salesman* do not dispute that the common man is a fit subject for tragedy but argue that Willy lacks stature, a charge Miller calls incredible but does not address. Instead, he proposes an alternative, the intensity of the tragic hero's commitment, which matters more than whether he falls from a great or small height, even than his consciousness of what is happening. 'The commonest of men may take on that stature to the extent of his willingness to throw all he has into the contest, the battle to secure his rightful place in his world.' By this criterion, Willy is a tragic hero. 'Tragedy, then, is the consequence of a man's total compulsion to evaluate himself justly.'

Because self-evaluation is what Willy is incapable of doing, some critics charge that he lacks the mental ability to become a tragic hero. But if Willy were unaware of his separation from enduring values, Miller argues, 'he would have died contentedly while polishing his car' as he listened to a baseball game on the radio. 'That he had not the intellectual fluency to verbalise his situation is not the same thing as saying that he lacked awareness.' While he does not know that he is 'as much the victim of his beliefs as their defeated exemplar', the audience does. Furthermore, in gaining the knowledge that his son loves him, 'he is given his existence, so to speak – his fatherhood, for which he has always striven'. To Miller, tragedy brings *us* knowledge and enlightenment – which it need not do for the tragic hero. In this respect, he may be more sophisticated than Aristotle, to whom thought or ideas are 'found where something is proved to be or not to be, or a general maxim is enunciated' (here and below, the S. H. Butcher translation of the *Poetics*, in Dukore).

From the evaluation of the individual in his environment comes the fear of diplacement from one's image of oneself in the world. To this, Miller links social criticism. If tragedy derives from a compulsion to evaluate oneself justly, then the destruction of the tragic hero posits an evil in his environment. Tragic enlightenment concerns this social wrong. But if society alone were responsible, the protagonist would have to be so faultless as to be incredible.

Thomas E. Porter claims that since Biff, supposedly knowing who he really is, advocates no more than a return to the farm, which is a cliché, the play lacks tragic epiphany, purgation and renewal. But as Murray notes, Biff speaks for Biff. The 'intellectual and moral confusion' found by Richard J. Foster (in Hurrell) apparently derives from an effort to locate an authorial spokesman. Let us start another question with 'What if'. What if Miller were to revise the play so that Willy fully understood his errors? The play would then become too explicit and Willy the know-it-all protagonist of a drama with Uplift. In addition, as Brian Parker notes, while Biff's self knowledge may not amount to much, its admission of limitation and weakness is the beginning of truth that 'in religious terms . . . would be called humility', and the Requiem permits the audience to associate Biff's acceptance with Willy's death

v. false pride

'as a single, coherent, and . . . tragic experience' (in Corrigan, *Miller*).

But Miller need not dispute Aristotle to stake a claim for his play as tragedy. According to Aristotle, 'Character is that which reveals moral purpose, showing what kind of things a man chooses or avoids'. Actually, Miller echoes this passage when he declares that it is necessary in tragedy to show not only why a person does what he does but also why he cannot refuse to do it. To adapt Miller's phrase about *A View from the Bridge*, Willy is incapable of settling for half. Charley's and Bernard's advice to forget Biff and to walk away recalls that of Jocasta, Ismene and Chrysothemis to let matters be and not push them to extremes. Like Oedipus, Antigone and Electra, Willy is incapable of walking away. His refusal to avoid full commitment is a mark of stature that links him to these Sophoclean heroes. Linda's inability to understand why Willy should kill himself is a mark of her incomprehension, not Miller's. 'No man only needs a little salary', says Charley, echoing Lear's 'reason not the need!' Like Lear, Willy is happy when he reconciles with the child he loves most.

Aristotle's definition of tragedy focuses on action: 'Tragedy, then, is an imitation of an action that is serious, complete and of a certain magnitude; in language embellished with each kind of artistic ornament, the several kinds being found in separate parts of the play; in the form of action, not of narrative; through pity and fear affecting the proper purgation of these emotions'. While I do not expect to resolve centuries of dispute in a single paragraph, let me try to relate these terms to *Death of a Salesman*. As Miller says, the action it attempts to imitate is Willy's effort to achieve his rightful status in the world – which, I would add, also means in his family. No one disputes the play's seriousness, and its completeness and magnitude follow Aristotle's dictum that they comprise a sequence of probable or necessary events that permit a change of fortune – in this case, from good to bad (death). According to Aristotle, imitation not verse distinguishes tragedy, and while the iambic metre is most appropriate to tragic dialogue, the reason is that it is the most colloquial, which Miller's play is. *Death of a Salesman* is certainly in the form of action, not narrative, even its exposition being dramatised rather than told. Unmerited misfortune, says Aristotle, arouses pity (Willy is a victim of society's false gods), the misfortune of someone like us arouses fear (one needs no further documentation of Willy's representativeness). His misfortunes derive not from vice or depravity but from what Butcher translates with appropriate ambiguity as error or frailty.

The plot is what Aristotle calls complex rather than simple: it contains a reversal and a recognition that accompany the protagonist's change of fortune. Both occur when Biff makes his father understand he loves him. Willy is '*astonished*' and thereby '*elevated*'. Despite his suicide, he is as victorious as the traditional tragic heroes, for he gains what he truly wants and values, his son's love.

A mid-twentieth-century work, *Death of a Salesman* cannot be a purely Hellenic tragedy – though it contains the major aspects of that form. As August Wilhelm von Schlegel observes, 'The Pantheon is not more different from Westminster Abbey or the church of St. Stephen at Vienna, than the structure of a tragedy of Sophocles from a drama of Shakespeare' (in Dukore). *Death of a Salesman* conforms to W. H. Auden's view of a Christian tragedy (one derived historically from the world-views of Christianity, not necessarily one whose author believes in Christian dogma) in contrast to a Greek tragedy: first, that the Greek is 'the tragedy of necessity'; i.e., the feeling aroused in the spectator is "What a pity it had to be this way"' in contrast to the former, which is 'the tragedy of possibility, "What a pity it was this way when it might have been otherwise"'; second, while the flaw (as Auden regards it) in the Greek hero's character consists of 'the illusion of a man who knows himself strong and believes that nothing can shake that strength', the corresponding failing in Christian tragedy is the sin of Pride, 'the illusion of a man who knows himself weak but believes he can by his own efforts transcend that weakness and become strong' (in Corrigan, *Tragedy*). To return to Schlegel, the true diagnostic of tragedy is that 'death stands everywhere in the background, and to it every well or ill-spent moment brings us nearer and closer'. From its outset, its very title, Miller's play conforms to this interpretation.

In G. W. F. Hegel's influential view, modern tragedy (i.e.

Shakespearean and after) differs from Grecian in that its all-important subject is 'the individual passion, the satisfaction of which can only be relative to a wholly personal end'. Subjectivity or self-assertion is more important than ethical ideals of family, church or state. *Hamlet* revolves around kingship, but the character of Hamlet, his individuality, is its focus (in Dukore). Similarly, no matter how much society is implicated, the focus of *Death of a Salesman* is on Willy Loman.

The drama of the bourgeoisie, modern drama has social dimensions different from those of its predecessors, says George Lukács, and it derives from 'conscious class confrontations'. In modern tragedy, the bad may not necessarily be replaced by the good, but it is replaced by something different in kind – in contrast to Shakespearean tragedy, wherein Hamlet and Claudius share the same moral outlook. 'The heroes of the new drama – in comparison to the old – are more passive than active; they are acted upon more than they act for themselves; they defend rather than attack; their heroism is mostly a heroism of anguish, of despair, not one of bold aggressiveness.' Lukács might well be describing *Death of a Salesman*, written 40 years later. The final battle of modern man, which modern tragedy dramatises, is within. Paradoxically, the hero not only has more internalised conflicts, he faces more external pressures than before. Modern tragedy is the tragedy of individualism. With the environment functioning as a dramatic element, individualism becomes problematic. Previously, man understood his place within a world order; now his place has become tenuous and the realisation of individual personality the subject of drama. Whereas tragedy was formerly brought on by the particular direction taken by the will, the mere act of willing now suffices. Without a mythology, 'the basis on which everything may be justified is character' (in Dukore). Dramatising the problematic nature of individualism and the pressures exerted by society, *Death of a Salesman* is based on the struggle of a character to realise himself.

THE CRUCIBLE

Just as critics were quick to note the dramatic antecedents of

Death of a Salesman, so did they lose little time in pointing out those of *The Crucible*, particularly Bernard Shaw's *Saint Joan*, whose protagonist is tried by religious authorities, confesses but tears up the recantation (which the historical John Proctor did not do) and undergoes martyrdom. The theme of individual conscience in defiance of authority is older than both plays. Its ancestry includes *An Enemy of the People*, on which Shaw had written and which Miller had adapted, and *Antigone*.

8   Witch Hunts

Roots of *The Crucible* include witch hunts in both twentieth and seventeenth-century America.

Miller admits that the genesis of *The Crucible* was the rise of McCarthyism (the term embraces the anti-Communist hysteria of both the Senate, where Joseph McCarthy chaired a subcommittee, and the House of Representatives Un-American Activities Committee or HUAC). The political right wing in America, he explains (Introduction to *Collected Plays*), created a reign of terror and a virtually holy mystique as people confessed, sought forgiveness of sins, and accepted the idea that 'conscience was no longer a private matter but one of state administration'.

Passages in *The Crucible* reverberate with the political atmosphere of the early 1950s. Proctor demands why Hale does not ask whether the accuser is blameless, and when Judge Danforth threatens to cite Giles Corey for contempt of court, Corey replies in terms that echo witnesses at HUAC: 'This is a hearing; you cannot clap me for contempt of a hearing'. Although no character anachronistically invokes the Fifth Amendment's protection against self-incrimination, Corey insists on his right to remain silent rather than inadvertently accuse himself – a right that Puritans exercised in seventeenth-century England and America. At the play's first performance, seven years after the Nuremberg Trials, where Nazis offered the excuse that they were functionaries who had to obey orders, audiences recognised the justification of the functionary come to arrest Elizabeth Proctor, 'I must do as I'm told'.

Except for the Communist *Daily Worker*, the daily press, perhaps fearful of identifying McCarthyism with witch-hunting, did not explicitly mention Communism, liberals under siege or McCarthyism. Because its action, says Walter Kerr, has 'a very clear contemporary parallel', it 'lives not in the warmth of humbly observed human souls but in the ideological heat of polemic' (*New York Herald Tribune*, 23 Jan. 1953), but he cites no parallel. Although Brooks Atkinson reaches a different conclusion – 'Mr. Miller is not pleading a cause in dramatic form' – he too is imprecise, citing only 'certain similarities between the perversions of justice then and today' (*New York Times*, 23 Jan. 1953). By contrast, the weekly journals were not timorous. The most influential review, by Eric Bentley (*New Republic*, 16 Feb. 1953, revised in Weales, *Crucible*), questions the validity of the parallel. Unlike witchcraft,

> communism is not . . . merely a chimera. The word communism is used to cover, first, the politics of Marx, second, the politics of the Soviet Union, and, third, the activities of all liberals as they seem to illiberal illiterates. Since Mr. Miller's argument bears only on the third use of the word, its scope is limited. Indeed, the analogy between 'red-baiting' and witch hunting can seem complete only to communists, for only to them is the menace of communism as fictitious as the menace of witches. The non-communist will look for certain reservations and provisos. In *The Crucible*, there are none.

Without mentioning Bentley, Miller's stage directions respond to him. In Communist countries, he says, ideological resistance 'is linked to the totally malign capitalist succubi, and in America any man who is not reactionary in his views is open to the charge of allegiance with the Red hell'. Once a government equates a political policy with morality and opposition to such policy with 'diabolical malevolence', its main role 'changes from that of the arbiter to that of the scourge of God'. No analogy is complete in all details. Bentley stresses where the parallel breaks down, Miller where it holds.

For this play, Miller examined historical documents. He altered some facts, mainly compressing the number of characters (girls, judges, witnesses), making the girls dance *naked* in the woods (the better to impress a 1953 audience), raising Abigail's age to seventeen (the girls, who in those days might marry at fourteen, were between sixteen and twenty), and inventing the affair between Proctor and Abigail (psychologically plausible for characters and audience). Essentially, though, *The Crucible* is historically accurate.

9 LANGUAGE

Some critics charge Miller with what John Simon calls 'linguistic insufficiency', concocting 'a pidgin-Colonial to make your eardrums buckle' (*New York*, 15 May 1972). For the most part, however, appraisals tend to agree with Julius Novick's, that the dialogue 'feels' historically accurate and 'can rise at times to a considerable level of eloquence' (*Village Voice*, 4 May 1972). English reviewers were more fulsome in their praise of the play's language before their American colleagues were. T. C. Worsley, who called *Death of a Salesman* 'Poetry without Words', applauded the language of *The Crucible*, 'which very successfully places us in the past without being either awkwardly archaic or falsely poetic' (*New Statesman and Nation*, 20 Nov. 1954). Kenneth Tynan admired the 'mastery of period dialogue. The prose is gnarled, whorled in its gleaming as a stick of polished oak' (*Observer*, 14 Nov. 1954).

Miller has invented a language that suggests the play's time and place. As he said in an interview, his use of words like 'poppet' instead of 'doll' and syntax like 'he have' instead of 'he has' reminds audiences that the play is set in a different period but is not difficult to understand, which it might be if he had 'used all the old language with words like "dafter" instead of "daughter"' (*Saturday Review*, 31 Jan. 1953). He echoes seventeenth-century sources, such as William Blake ('no man knows when the harlots' cry will end his life'), Ben Jonson ('A fart on Thomas Putnam') and virtually any Restoration comedy ('They're gulling you, Mister!'). The language evokes the Bible ('now remember what the angel

Raphael said to the boy Tobias'), rings with the sounds of the hellfire and brimstone pulpit ('it's death drivin' into them, forked and hoofed'), uses zesty colloquial imagery ('your justice would freeze beer'), has a homespun rhetoric ('I have gone tiptoe in this house all seven months since she is gone. I have not moved from there to there without I think to please you, and still an everlasting funeral marches round your heart') and can vary within fairly tight boundaries, as in the colour changes that move from suggesting the angelic to the diabolic: Parris asks Abigail whether her reputation is entirely white; she responds that there is no blush (red) about it and replies, when he says that Elizabeth seems to think she might be soiled (grey), that she will not blacken her face for anyone.

Because the idiom is unfamiliar, says Penelope Curtis in the play's most extensive linguistic analysis (in Weales, *Crucible*), Miller is better able to heighten it. 'The result is that if he cannot create his themes in the language, as Shakespeare does, he can do the next best thing: use his language to suggest and support them.' The rhetoric is individualised: John Proctor's has a pulpit-like, sometimes bombastic 'tone of righteous fury', whereas his wife's is drawn 'more from the common ethic'. The phrases reveal character, as Parris's having 'fought here three long years to bend these stiff-necked people to me' – his own stiff-necked qualities emerging from his harsh, determined speech. Also, Curtis observes, the lively play of 'half-metaphor' suggests that what he considers obstinacy in others is upright in himself, and the 'blend of ugliness and resonance in his language' conveys 'just how far he is typical of the others, and how far his feelings are extreme ones'.

Because the Salem community was so closely knit, she says, its concerns so interwoven, such terms as *name* carry a cluster of associations including salvation, reputation, prestige and pride. Nevertheless, one must agree with Ruby Cohn (in Martin) that despite its felicities the language is not free of blemishes. Observing how 'the moral choices turn upon the simple word *name*', Cohn notes that Abigail assures her uncle that there is no taint upon hers, that the witch hunters shift the idea of a good name to that of naming names, that Corey foreshadowing Proctor preserves his name by refusing to name others, that Miller partly anchors Proctor's abstractions in the word *name*, that by confessing to adultery he tarnishes his name and stains Abigail's, that to save his name Elizabeth lies about his adultery, and that after declaring God has seen his name on his confession and begging 'I have given you my soul; leave me my name!' he understands that 'his soul and his name are virtually synonymous'. Unfortunately, she adds, in Proctor's sanctimonious last words 'The shift from "name" to "honour" weakens his heroics'.

10   Authority and the Individual

Among the major themes of *The Crucible* is the conflict between authority and the individual who dissents from its demands and restrictions. In seventeenth-century Salem, authority was willingly accepted, not imposed, as a social necessity. Having fled religious persecution in England, the Massachusetts Puritans were wary of persecution in the New World. They closed ranks to support a unified society that, under God, promised safety. Life was harsh (of the 103 Mayflower passengers who landed at Plymouth on 21 December 1620, only half survived the first winter) and the presence of Indians in surrounding forests was still a danger (Abigail watched them kill her parents and Proctor carries a rifle when he plants his crops). Small wonder that the Salemites, their religion synthesising fears of the wild and pagan forest, considered it to be the Devil's preserve. Because Salem was a theocratic state, every religious or secular transgression offended both domains. As Danforth states, Salem's law is based on the Bible, which, 'writ by Almighty God, forbid the practice of witchcraft, and describe death as the penalty thereof'; also, 'the law and Bible damn all bearers of false witness'.

Although Proctor says, 'I like not the smell of this "authority"', he refers to Putnam's landgrabbing and Parris's leadership. Like other Salemites, like most Americans, he respects the authority of law, which he does not condemn until the end of Act III, but as he learns, authority that fails to consider individuals has a diabolical stench. Thus, the individual is morally obliged to dissent – at whatever the cost.

The fear of witchcraft permitted the release of repressed sexual fantasies and fears (a possessed spirit lay with the accuser), social hostilities (someone who had unjustly acquired property was under diabolical influence), class antagonisms and anxieties (toward slaves and the poor), not to mention overt sexual desire (Abigail) and economic greed (Putnam). Miller skilfully interweaves the social and the sexual or personal. Whereas Proctor is in his mid-thirties, Abigail is half his age. Miller does not stress this disparity – perhaps to avoid making the play primarily about a middle-aged lecher and an adolescent girl – but instead emphasises guilt. For Proctor, remorse not passion is the keynote.

Connections between sex and society manifest themselves early and continue toward the end. In Act I, Abigail becomes sexually aroused when Proctor enters. She tries to excite him: '*feverishly looking into his eyes*' with '*concentrated desire*', she reminds him how he clutched her behind his house and 'sweated like a stallion' when she approached. As the play develops, her personal desires change. The climax of Act III is not possession by sexual passion but by demons. Furthermore, Abigail is in only two of the four acts. Whereas the sexual triangle might compete with the social drama early in the play, it gives way to the wider issues as the play develops. By the final act, the social aspect dominates – the sound of bellowing cows wandering the roads because their jailed masters cannot milk them, the stress on whether the community has faith in the court, the need to gain confessions from imprisoned dissenters. Even Elizabeth's confession of complicity in John's adultery is subordinated to the social ramifications of his conduct. His integrity in admitting one (adultery) foreshadows his integrity in denying the other (witchcraft).

With others too, the personal and the social connect. Whereas Thomas Putnam thinks to acquire land from those hanged for witchcraft, his wife wants to uncover the reason (diabolical, she is certain) that seven of her children died in infancy and the eighth lies sick. Actually, witchcraft generated the girls' illness and the later deviltry that occurred in Salem, for Ann Putnam bade her daughter persuade Tituba to conjure the spirits of her dead infants.

A major difference between *The Crucible* and *Death of a Salesman* is that the characters of the former are more conscious of and articulate about ethical considerations than those of the latter. As indicated, the meanings of *name* include reputation, honesty and integrity. In Salem, name in all three senses was a dominant moral factor. When Abigail cries out for her good name, she hypocritically asks for a reputation she does not merit – much like Eddie in *A View from the Bridge*. But whereas her and Eddie's names depend on the approval of others, Proctor's name depends on his own existential valuation. His decision to win his life by pleading guilty of witchcraft derives from his view that as he has broken one commandment, a lie will not further stain a soul already filthy. Although he wants his wife to approve this decision, she will not do so: he himself, she says, must judge. When he finds himself unable to utter lies that may influence others toward evil, he recognises some goodness within. True to his essential self, he accepts both guilt and virtue, claims his integrity, or *name*, and goes to the gallows to preserve what is best in him.

11 CHARACTERS

Unlike *Death of a Salesman*, *The Crucible* has a large number of characters. Responding to evil and to personal danger, each enters his own crucible, thereby testing his integrity. As protagonist, John Proctor exemplifies the tensions between self-preservation and integrity. At first, Elizabeth is so unforgiving and unyielding that integrity about her marriage becomes a vice; later, she admits her own complicity in her husband's deed. Lacking integrity, Abigail accuses others in order to save herself. Like Elizabeth, Hale moves from one position to another. Beginning with integrity (open-mindedness about the possibility of witches in Salem), he ends by abjuring integrity (to save one's life, one should lie). But as Murray points out, no single character represents the author's view of the right path. Although Elizabeth praises Proctor's decision to die, she would also praise his decision to live. Hale is unconverted by Proctor's action, as is Danforth, who has his own integrity (he wants a confession to justify his deeds but refuses to accept a lie).

One way to regard the characters is through the lens of authority. Land and wealth give it to the Putnams, to whom the ostensible religious leader Parris defers to prop his position. Hale's academic authority proves of little use beside Danforth's judicial authority. Proctor, Corey and Rebecca Nurse set themselves against authority. While the play contains 'bad' and 'good' Salemites of varying degrees, each group has one basic representative, Abigail and Rebecca, and one who wavers, Mary and Hale.

Their virtue and vice are partly defined by what they fear and their response to it. Abigail and Tituba fear punishment; the former first blames the latter but both blame the Devil and those seduced by the Fiend. Parris fears loss of his position (by Putnam at the start, the populace at the end); to keep it, he allies himself with the powerful and condemns scapegoats. Ann Putnam fears sterility; to overcome it, she would ally herself with Satan. Failing to see the hypocrisy of trafficking with the Devil to learn of his influence in destroying her babes before they lived to be baptised, she accuses others of doing what she did. While Parris is at first '*horrified*' to learn of her actions, he soon adjusts – in contrast to Rebecca Nurse, also '*horrified*', who does not. Just as the vicious characters employ guilt by association, so does Miller, who associates the virtuous characters with each other. Though Cory has no hand in Proctor's actions at the end of Act III, Miller connects them by having Danforth order both to be taken to jail after Proctor's outburst declaring God to be dead. Continuing to employ virtue by association, Miller then has Hale denounce the proceedings and quit the court.

Most of the play's comedy is unintentional on the part of the characters. Before Parris leaves his unconscious daughter in order to lead the villagers in a psalm, he orders Abigail to send for him if his daughter tries to fly out the window. Apart from the preposterous command, the audience sees a fuddy-duddy, frightened little man execute the standard comic technique of cross-and-turn-back. Comically ironic, Ann Putnam enters '*full of breath, shiny-eyed*' as if to declare something good, but instead she announces 'a stroke of hell' upon the minister. With comic incongruity, Corey is eager to see the inert Betty Parris fly. Hale sees no comic self-contradiction, or even irony, in scholarly tomes that aim to define, codify and callibrate an admittedly invisible world. When Elizabeth declares that she had never before heard Mary Warren charge that Goody Osburn had often tried to kill her, Mary innocently responds that she never before realised it. Martha Corey replies, when asked how she knows she is not a witch if she does not know what a witch is, that if she were one she would know it. Giles Corey, who had been a plaintiff in court 33 times, is surprised that Danforth's father, also a judge, did not tell him of the time 35 years earlier when he awarded Corey £9 in damages.

As Walter Meserve notes (in Martin), intentional comedy links the virtuous characters to each other, since only they use it. Corey explicitly makes the connection when he refers to Proctor and himself as 'this fool and I'. The principal wit or ironist is Proctor, whose first speech ends with comic irony (a complaint that he is looking for his servant Mary Warren more often than for his cows) and whose second begins with humorous profanity (when Mary protests she wanted to see great doings in the world, he promises to show her great doings on her arse). Rebecca Nurse's wit associates her with Proctor. To Ann Putnam's assertion that because her daughter cannot eat she must be bewitched, Rebecca suggests she may not be hungry. Soon, after Parris demanding more money for his services points out that he is a graduate of Harvard, Corey concludes that he has been well instructed in arithmetic. Proctor connects with such joke-making by declaring that at the last church meeting he attended Parris spoke so much about deeds and mortgages, he thought he was at an auction.

John Proctor Despite the impression that Proctor is sceptical enough to perceive from the start the truth behind the crying-out of witchcraft, the fact is that once he and Abigail are alone, she dismisses the notion of witchcraft as tosh and confides to him part of the truth about Betty Parris's illness. He is not as good as Rebecca, he wavers before committing himself to a course of action, and he is sufficiently unvirtuous to have had an affair with a teenager. He is physically but not morally strong (if the *strikingly beautiful* Abigail's behaviour in the play is an indication, she may have been the one to take the initiative). Although he does not like the smell of authority, in his phrase, the odour bothers him only when others exert it over him: he does not hesitate to use it upon his servant, to whom he brandishes a whip. As Miller says, Proctor is not only a sinner against the morality of his time, he sins against his own view of decency. Instead of a virtuous man exercising his virtue, he is a troubled soul who discovers, to his surprise, that he has virtue. He rejects the advances of Abigail, who would rekindle his ardour, but he is less than open with his wife, to whom he lies about Abigail (they had been alone together) and about Elizabeth's cooking (he added salt to the food: their marriage lacks this and other spices). Unlike Willy Loman, he evaluates himself justly. His guilt of adultery links to his innocence of witchcraft. He recognises that despite his sinfulness his nature makes him refuse to commit an unjust act (to agree to the posting of his signed confession would make him an exemplar of a lie and, as the play reiterates, God damns all liars). Thus, he can die with honour and goodness, albeit only a shred, which suffices to give him self-respect.

Reverend John Hale   Unlike Proctor, Reverend Hale ends with less stature than he begins. While he expresses misgivings about the trials to the Proctors, he believes the Devil is a real enemy. Though suspicious that the condemned confess to avoid being hanged, he tries to maintain his faith in the court, for the Church is the foundation of his life. With Elizabeth's arrest and Mary's hearing, his doubts about the reliability of the witnesses accumulate until he concludes that Proctor, not Abigail, is truthful. After he denounces the court, he subverts his clerical office by counselling the condemned to lie, for he hopes God damns liars less than those who throw away His most precious gift, life, for pride. Elizabeth calls his reasoning diabolical. Ironically, his belief that to die for nothing does no good is close to today's common viewpoint.

Giles Corey Like Proctor, Corey goes to his death heroically. Unlike Proctor, he is not hanged. Since he would be hanged and his property auctioned if he responded to the charges, he neither confirms nor denies them. When the authorities lay large stones upon his chest, his only words are 'More weight'. Whereas Proctor dies for a principle, his righteous name, Corey dies as he lives, for property: as silence would qualify him for Christian burial, his property would go to his sons.

Rebecca Nurse Like Proctor a force that represents the good, Rebecca also resembles him in a modern outlook. His transgression and guilt draw sympathy from contemporary audiences. Her understanding of children is more closely allied to our time than to hers. Dismissing the notion that they are bewitched by the Devil, this mother of eleven observes that the 'silly seasons' of youngsters enable them to 'run the Devil bowlegged' and that patience will enable one to catch a child's spirit, which through love will return of its own accord. When she hears that Hale might try to exorcise the Demon from Betty Parris's body, this godly woman's only concern is that the child might be hurt. When in the last act Proctor confesses to witchcraft, she hopes God will show mercy to him for having lied. Since to lie would be to damn her soul, she refuses to confess. Miller does not overemphasise her goodness but establishes her as a rebuke to the madness of others and a goal towards which Proctor may aspire.

Elizabeth Proctor Sensitive enough to feel sad to have killed a rabbit, who had wandered into the house, for supper, Elizabeth is initially cold, unforgiving and uncharitable towards her formerly unfaithful husband. Rightly, critics have made much of the crucial scene of Act III wherein to save her husband's reputation she lies about his adultery. What requires notice is that in doing so she contrasts with Abigail, for Elizabeth lies to *save* another's life, and that in Act IV, she confesses guilt – an *honest* confession, in contrast to the one Danforth tempts Proctor to make, which helps to solder the private and public areas of the play. Recognising her own sins, she admits that a cold wife is required to provoke adultery. Whereas she fails to forgive him in Act II, she begs him to forgive her in Act IV. Like Linda Loman, she has the last words in the play. Her final speech, proclaiming Proctor's goodness, brings a note of triumph to his death.

Abigail Williams   Partly a malign parody of the seduced and abandoned orphan, Abigail is a passionate young woman with unsatiated sexual needs. She condemns Elizabeth for coldness. A forceful personality, Abigail is able to bend the other girls to her will and intelligent enough to convince the pillars of society of her truthfulness. At a polar extreme from Rebecca Nurse, she is the most evil person in the play, who would kill to gain the man for whom she lusts. Initially impelled by the twin motives of lust for Proctor and desire for self-preservation, both motives turn to lust for power.

Deputy Governor, Judge Danforth   Since Judge Danforth is convinced of his cause's justice and his own probity, he takes an assault on the court to be an attack on himself. He is sufficiently honest that he wavers when it appears that Mary may be telling the truth, but he wonders whether Proctor may unconsciously desire to undermine the court, for he himself has seen people choked by spirits. It makes sense to summon Elizabeth to verify her husband's admission of adultery with Abigail, who denies the charge. When in the final act Danforth tries to exact a confession from Proctor, he insists that it is not a lie to save his life. However blinded he may be, Danforth's religious convictions are sincere (though no less insidious than Abigail's actions).

Reverend Samuel Parris   A weak, mean-spirited man, Parris believes himself to be persecuted by enemies, and since he sincerely tries to win them to godliness, he cannot understand why people resist him. Though a minister, his chief concern is less God than his authority. If his daughter trafficked with spirits in the heathen forest, then his enemies may use her action to ruin him. Deferential towards the powerful, he is a petty tyrant to the helpless Black slave Tituba, at whom he screams as soon as she enters the room. Terrified that his home may be associated with diabolical influences, he is relieved when Hale suggests that if this be the case it is because the Devil wants to subvert the best. Only apparently does he reverse himself in Act IV. Then as before, he aims to save himself, for the populace, now opposed to the witch-hunters, has threatened him. But he is not a cardboard villain. His suspicion that the girls conjured evil spirits proves justified. Although Proctor scores off him comically for his demand that he have the deed to his house, he is Salem's third preacher in seven years and fears being 'put out like the cat whenever some majority feels the whim'.

Tituba   A reminder of rigid class divisions in Salem (Proctor behaves towards Mary much as Parris does towards Tituba), the Barbados slave also parallels Abigail. When Paris threatens Tituba with whipping and Putnam threatens her with hanging, she acts upon Abigail's example. She pleads that she was an unwilling accomplice of the Devil and that someone else bewitched the girls. Unable to imagine whom to identify as witches, she is wily enough to verify names suggested by others.

12   DRAMATIC STRUCTURE

Whereas the structure of *Death of a Salesman* is compact in the Ibsenite or Hellenic manner, that of *The Crucible* is panoramic in the Shakespearean manner, requiring relatively little exposition at the start. The play divides into two parts, each with two acts. Both involve integrity, which dominates the second part, wherein Proctor confesses to adultery, the private sin (Act III), and denies witchcraft, the public sin (Act IV). Despite the fusion of private and public spheres in both parts, the settings of the first are private residences (Parris's and Proctor's homes), of the second public arenas (trial room and jail cell). These locales mirror the thematic concerns, which moving outwards towards the public arena suggest a broadening of scope to embrace the Massachusetts colony.

Each act has a major motif and contrast between beginning and end. The chief motif of Act I is the attempt to find blame for both private and public problems; physical illness becomes a sign of moral illness, thus of the battle between God and the Devil. Whereas Act I begins with prayer, it ends with ecstatic cries about the Devil. The central motif of Act II is the court's gradual invasion of the Proctor home. Quasi-judicial hearings turn from the private to the public. The act begins with John Proctor returning home; it ends with his wife leaving. At the start, they are physically together yet emotionally separated; at the end, physically separated yet emotionally united, as he prepares to risk his reputation to save her life. Act III's dominant motif is the establishment of the credibility of accuser and accused. It opens with an offstage voice charging a woman with witchcraft, which she denies; it closes with a man charged with working for the Devil, but instead of denying it he calls everyone in the room, including himself, guilty. Confession of guilt is the principal motif of the final act. In contrast with the first, the blame is of oneself rather than others. Whereas Elizabeth confesses herself guilty of her husband's adultery, he confesses to witchcraft but recants his confession. Act IV begins with people drinking spirits and joking about the Devil; it ends with a man affirming his virtue by going through death to God.

The first scenic unit of Act I primarily concerns Parris and Abigail. The doctor's report that Betty's illness may be attributable to unnatural causes involves an effort to avoid taking blame (for ignorance to a cure). When Parris is terrified that the doctor may be correct, Abigail decisively orders the messenger to remain silent. Like Parris, she wants to keep this public issue private. When he questions her about what happened in the woods, she gives excuses and false oaths.

Admitting the girls danced, she denies they conjured spirits, calls Tituba's invocations Barbados songs and swears no one was naked. In the second scenic unit, superstition and rumour enter with the Putnams. When Ann reveals that her daughter Ruth joined the girls to conjure the dead to learn why Ann's children died in infancy, Abigail covers her lie with another: she herself did no conjuring, Tituba and Ruth did. Anticipating later developments, which include Hale's efforts to persuade the condemned to lie (immoral means) to save their lives (a righteous end), Ann tried to commune with infernal spirits (evil means) to beget children who will live (a righteous end).

Alone for the first time, the girls reveal the truth. Abigail's influence over them foreshadows her ability to influence the court. To ensure that everyone tells the same story, she explains what the others know and do not know. She brutally shakes Betty and threatens to beat her. Terrified, Betty darts from the bed, calling for her dead mother. The effect of conversations about witchcraft on a susceptible adolescent girl foreshadows what will occur in court. Though inert, Betty has subliminally absorbed the conversation. To fly to her mother, she tries to leave through the window, then reveals another lie of Abigail, who drank blood as a charm to kill Elizabeth.

When Proctor is alone with Abigail, we learn that they had committed adultery but that he, unlike she, determines not to resume their affair. Insisting she wipe their relationship from her mind, he declares that they never touched each other. As he will discover, repentance does not come so easily. Furthermore, his statement is a lie and, as the play reiterates, God damns liars.

As a crowd scene follows their intimate scene, personal sin (adultery) connects to public sin (witchcraft). Parishioners downstairs sing a psalm, Abigail attempts to entice Proctor sexually and Betty screams. Led by Parris, the singers rush into the room. Ann Putnam concludes that since Betty began to scream when she heard the psalm, it must be because she could not bear God's name.

Hale's entry signals another impulse in the dramatic action, another stage in the motif of blame. His questioning draws further admissions from Abigail, who to save herself blames others: there was soup and a frog jumped into it, she did not

call the Devil but Tituba did, she and Betty drank none of
the brew but Tituba tried to make her do so, she and Betty
drank blood but at Tituba's instigation, Tituba's spirit came
to her at church to make her laugh at prayer, Tituba appeared
while she slept and denuded her. Taking her cue from Abigail's
denial of guilt and blame of others as witches, Tituba absolves
herself by naming others. As though inspired and enraptured,
Abigail begs to return to Jesus, confirms Tituba's names and
adds another. With increasing theatrical momentum, the girls
cite more names. On their ecstatic shrieks, the act ends.

Structurally, the major thrust of the second act is the
intrusion of the court into the Proctor home until the Proctors
are separated. Initially, their major concern is private. John
tries to placate Elizabeth but she merely '*receives*' his kiss.
Their apartness is visualised: he stands by the doorway, his
back to her, she by the basin, her back to him, the room
between them. The invasion of the court into their home
begins when she discloses that their servant Mary is now an
official of the court, which has imprisoned fourteen people,
whom it might hang. Their discussion of his infidelity employs
legal terminology. He urges her to judge him no longer, as if
their home were a courtroom, declares he will no longer plead
his honesty, and recalls he had confessed his transgression to
her. She asserts that a magistrate in his own heart judges him.

The public court further intrudes when Mary returns
from Salem to disclose more arrests, a death sentence, and
(foreshadowing) the court's view that inability to remember
the ten commandments is proof of guilt. Although she gives
Elizabeth a doll she made in court that day, she discloses that
Elizabeth was mentioned – evidence to the prescient wife that
Abigail wants her dead so she may replace her. Whereas the
court has entered the Proctor home, Elizabeth wants her
husband to enter the court to tell the truth about Abigail.

As a witch-hunter in a theocratic state, Hale arrives on
court business, for which he uses an obvious euphemism:
questions about the home's Christian character. When Proctor
can recite only nine commandments, Elizabeth prompts the
tenth, the injunction against adultery. Ineffectively, he tries
to joke his forgetfulness away with the quip that between them
they know all ten. When Elizabeth asks him to tell Hale the

truth about the girls' accusations, he repeats what Abigail had told him on the day Hale arrived. Hale reluctantly admits to a misgiving that some confessed for fear of being hanged if they denied the charge.

As in Act I, a crowd scene climaxes Act II. Apart from the theatrical effectiveness of a large number of people following a small number, the crowd helps give Proctor stature, since it congregates at his home, as if he were a leader (for a person of low rank, this is like a king's court in seventeenth-century drama). This sequence more openly discusses the proceedings of the court, which private vengeance uses for its own ends. Cheever represents the court's official entry into the Proctor home, since he is a clerk who has come with a warrant to arrest Elizabeth, charged by Abigail with trying to kill her by sticking needles in a doll. After Elizabeth's arrest, Proctor forces Mary to join him in denouncing Abigail in court, despite the possibility that his adultery will be revealed. Private and public terms of trial merge and Mary's repeated declaration 'I cannot' anticipates important developments in the next act.

In Act III, the play moves into the courtroom, a public arena that deliberates public guilt but where private guilt will also emerge. Whereas the act concludes with a full courtroom, it starts with an empty room. For a full page, one hears offstage voices. When a prisoner and a court official enter, the terror of the court invades the room visually as well as vocally. Early argument foreshadows the act's major motif, the establishment of the truthfulness of accuser and accused. While the girls assert that the upright Rebecca Nurse sent her spirit to murder seven babes, argues Proctor, one of them will swear she lied. The accused Elizabeth has claimed to be pregnant, which would spare her life, but though Judge Danforth is sceptical, Proctor insists she never lies.

Did Proctor threaten Mary to make her sign the deposition? To help determine whether Mary lied then or now, Danforth questions Abigail, who denies Mary's claim that she saw her make the doll in court and stick a needle into it for safekeeping. Proctor accuses her of trying to murder his wife, he cites her removal from church for laughter during prayers, and when he accuses her of having led the other girls to the woods at night to dance naked, Hale confirms that Parris had told him these facts when he arrived in Salem. If as Mary claims she pretended to turn cold and have an icy skin, let her now demonstrate the truth of this assertion, the court demands. Repeating what she reiterated at the end of Act II, Mary simply says she cannot. She is unable to explain why.

To Danforth's query as to whether she might have been mistaken about seeing spirits, Abigail responds with indignation, a warning of hell's powers, and an enactment of what Mary had called pretence. Claiming a cold wind has descended, she acts frightened. Through chattering teeth, she asks why Mary, her accuser, has done this. Echoing her words at the end of Act II, Mary hysterically cries that she cannot.

To destroy Abigail's credibility, knowing that he will also destroy himself, Proctor interrupts, calls her a whore and confesses to adultery. To prove his truthfulness, also foreshadowing his concern at the end, he points out that a man will not easily relinquish his good name. Elizabeth, he says, dismissed Abigail from their employ because of adultery.

What follows has been variously called one of those 'tricky twists of plot that Sardou himself might have admired' (Julius Novick, *Village Voice*, 4 May 1972) and 'no mere trick of melodrama' for it grows 'from a character' (Philip Hope-Wallace, *Manchester Guardian*, 11 April 1956). Elizabeth, who Proctor had insisted is incapable of lying – is brought to confirm his accusation. In a theatrically vivid moment, Danforth has Proctor and Abigail turn their backs to each other and instructs them not to speak to Elizabeth, whom he places between them. When Danforth asks why she dismissed Abigail, Elizabeth to save her husband's name hedges. Asked whether he is an adulterer, she lies for the same reason – which confirms Abigail and condemns him. Elizabeth thus enters her own purgatory, or crucible, from which she emerges in the next act.

Irrefutably reestablishing the credibility of the initial accuser, the previous arguments are theatricalised. With a bloodcurdling shriek, Abigail points to the ceiling and addresses a yellow bird. Apparently possessed, as in Act I, she and the other girls try to persuade the bird not to attack them for doing God's work. First Abigail, then all the girls repeat Mary's statements. Verbal and nonverbal unite. Demanding they stop pretending, Mary stamps her feet, then raises her fists; they repeat demand, stamp and gesture. The girls rush about, fearful of a swooping bird, until Mary, '*as though infected*', screams with them. Gradually, Abigail and the others stop, until only Mary stares at the bird, madly screaming. She accuses Proctor of being the Devil's instrument, asserts that he wants her name and accuses him of trying to overthrow the court. When Danforth charges Proctor with joining the Antichrist, he denounces the court. Then Hale does – a different kind of echo from the previous one.

Three months precede the last act. The prison and cemetery population has increased, with the result that orphans wander the town, abandoned cattle bellow, crops rot and people fear that they may become victims of the court. Rebellion against the courts, which has broken out in nearby Andover, threatens Salem.

The start of Act IV is a distorting mirror of the start of Act I. In Act I, a girl sleeps and a minister prays in vain to waken her; in Act IV, Sarah Good and Tituba sleep and a jailer succeeds in waking them. Instead of invoking God, as the minister does in Act I, the women invoke the Devil. Whereas the first act exposition reveals that the girls drank chicken blood, the fourth act has the women and their jailer drink cider and the Marshall enter almost drunk. Whereas characters in Act I deny traffic with the Devil, those in Act IV are anxious to join him, since Barbados and Hell are desirable places to fly to on so cold a day. Those who helped to establish guilt are revealed to be criminals; with Mercy, Abigail has run away after breaking into Parris's strongbox and stealing all his money.

Although Parris tries to persuade Danforth to postpone further executions until Hale has convinced someone to confess, Danforth refuses since to delay, reprieve or pardon might cast doubt on the guilt of those he has already had killed. His own reputation as an honest jurist, his name, has become more important than the basis of a good name. Ironically, evidence of Elizabeth's truthfulness arrives: she is well on in her pregnancy.

Since Proctor has not seen her for three months, Danforth and Parris think she might be instrumental in making him confess. Ironically, she confesses to him (provocation to commit adultery). Because his private sin initially prompts him to accept the same verdict for his public sin, he confesses to the latter. Recognising their differences, however, he renounces the confession to die with honour, goodness and name intact.

The foregoing analysis omits a scene Miller added six months after opening night. Inserted between the second and third acts, it has Proctor meet Abigail in the forest to warn her what he will do if she does not change her accusation of his wife. Abigail, who has come to believe her lies, cannot imagine he will confess. The chief advantage of the scene is psychological exploration of Abigail. Its disadvantages are interruption of the dramatic momentum from arrest to trial, overemphasis on the psychological and personal aspects of the play, diminution of the impact of Act III (with Abigail forewarned of what will happen) and weakening of credibility (would Proctor arrange a clandestine meeting with her on the eve of confessing their adultery?). Although the scene is not in *Collected Plays*, it appears as an Appendix to the Bantam paperback and in Weales's edition of text and commentary.

13 TRAGEDY?

Like *Death of a Salesman*, *The Crucible* aspires to tragedy. Frank Granville Barker remarks on its atmosphere of 'tragic horror' and its 'Hellenic inevitability' (*Plays and Players*, May 1954). Bernard Levin puns on Aristotle's *Poetics*: it 'tells with terror and pitilessness the story of one of the most terrible and pitiless aberrations mankind has ever suffered' (*Daily Mail*, 20 Jan. 1965). To John Gassner, Proctor has greater tragic stature than Willy Loman, and his death 'is on an obviously higher level of tragic sacrifice than Willy's suicide' (in Ferres). Even John Simon, who repeatedly savages *Death of a Salesman*, applauds the later play, accepting as psychologically and dramatically valid the relationship between Proctor's self-recognised guilt in 'a minor, expiated transgression' and his innocence in 'a major, social context', the former making him vulnerable to attacks concerning the latter, and he calls Proctor 'both an Aristotelian hero complete with *hamartia* and a Freudian hero made incomplete by a nagging sense of guilt' (*New York*, 15 May 1972).

Although *The Crucible* is controversial, most of those who refuse to bestow the mantle of tragedy on it regard it as a nontragic drama of great merit. 'If ever there were a work to dignify the name of melodrama', says Irving Wardle, 'it is this play' (*Times*, 31 Oct. 1980). To Harold Hobson, its failure 'to incorporate . . . the real strengths of Massachusetts Puritanism' and to reveal an 'awareness that such strengths exist' – in other words, to make a better case for Proctor's antagonists – 'reduces to a melodrama what might have been a true glimpse of tragic vision' (*Sunday Times*, 24 Jan. 1965). The most telling argument against *The Crucible* as tragedy is by Eric Bentley, who calls it a melodrama because the conflict is 'between the wholly guilty and the wholly innocent', and while the guilty may be as evil as Miller portrays them, the innocent is too pure; 'though the hero has weaknesses, he has no faults. His innocence is unreal because it is total', and impossible as well, for he cannot have committed the crime of which he is charged, commerce with the Devil (*New Republic*, 16 Feb. 1953; rpt in Weales, *Crucible*). To Bentley, the interweaving of witchcraft with Proctor's guilt about adultery is unrealised.

'I gotta use words when I talk to you', complains the title character of T. S. Eliot's *Sweeney Agonistes*. Therein lies one difficulty in dealing with such terms as tragedy and melodrama, since the former incorporates many of the latter's attributes. Cannot one consider Claudius's disruption of the performance of *The Murder of Gonzago* in *Hamlet* to be melodramatic? Similarly, the handkerchief motivation in *Othello*, the blinding of Gloucester in *King Lear* and the intensifying rage of Oedipus against the blind Tiresias in *Oedipus the King*? Certainly in terms of stage effectiveness, these scenes conform to what one usually considers melodramatic. Thus, the paradoxical but not self-contradictory comment by Robert Cushman that *The Crucible* 'is not melodramatic in its presentation of good and evil . . . but in its shape and tempo; it builds to a thrillingly organised trial scene in which life-

and-death debate gives way to fraudulent hysteria' (*Observer*, 5 March 1981).

Bigsby's analysis of *A View from the Bridge* suggests why, by contrast, *The Crucible* is not a melodrama. The former, he says, lacks 'self-conscious characters confronted with moral choices which are real because the alternatives which they face are equally available', and he adds, explaining Eddie's inadequacies as protagonist, that 'where there is no freedom there is no choice – where there is no choice there can be no culpability'. The factor of moral choice marks a distinction between melodrama and tragedy. In the former, heroes and villains have none: what they have been from the start determines their actions. In the latter, they continually define themselves by decisions and actions that have ethical alternatives. In *The Crucible*, Miller depicts, in his phrase, why the protagonist does what he does, or almost does not do so. Through self-examination, Proctor gains a better understanding of himself and his society; through that understanding he determines a course of action, which he undergoes. Decision and action, which Aristotelianly reveal moral worth, make him prefer to be the victim rather than the accomplice of evil. As his fate becomes an individual victory that affirms his moral position while it deprives those who kill him of vindication, it affects society. Thus too, his martyrdom represents a triumph, not only of himself as individual, but of the ethical forces he represents. All of these occur despite his personal guilt that makes him vulnerable. Furthermore, others bear witness to his decision and death: not only those who personify evil (Danforth and Parris) but also those who personify good (Elizabeth and Rebecca) and a pivotal figure (Hale). In addition, the seasonal movement in the play follows the tragic pattern, from springtime in Act I to autumn in Act IV – which Miller dramatises in costumes and dialogue. Yet the closing moment of the play is not bleak. Appropriate to the triumph of Proctor and what he represents, '*new sun*' pours on Elizabeth's face.

Unlike Willy Loman's fate, Proctor's involves the entire community. Curtis argues that *The Crucible* is close in spirit to Sophoclean tragedy, 'for the fate of the Salem people actually depends, to a lesser or greater extent, on the choices of individual men' and as in Sophocles 'the fate of the community involves more than the physical life or death of its members: there is a metaphysic at stake, and a way of life; the reputation of a people which becomes, by extension, an image of human possibilities' (in Weales, *Crucible*). Miller's choice of historical setting enables him to portray a protagonist and a community which are self-aware, conscious of principles of moral conflicts and conduct, and capable of articulation. As he says in his Preface to the one-act version of *A View from the Bridge*, an industrialised society like ours is so vast and complex that when one dramatises a hero 'our common sense reduces him to the size of a complainer, a misfit. . . . We have abstracted from the Greek drama its air of doom, its physical destruction of the hero, but its victory escapes us'. In *The Crucible*, which unlike *Death of a Salesman* and *A View from the Bridge* is not set in the present day, victory does not escape us.

PART TWO: PERFORMANCE

14 INTRODUCTION

However much the scenery, lighting and music used for the production of Miller's plays may depart from realism, the performance style usually does not: 'the actor's appearance on the stage in normal human guise leads us to expect a realistic treatment' (Introduction to *Collected Plays*). For example, when Miller redirected *The Crucible* six months after it first opened, at the same theatre, he replaced the pictorially realistic log cabin set with black curtains; but the acting style remained realistic. *Death of a Salesman* was first directed by Elia Kazan and its first Willy was Lee J. Cobb, both alumni of the Group Theatre, which in the 1930s brought the Stanislavsky system of acting to America. Many members of that first company belonged to the Actor's Studio, which derived from the Group and whose guru was a cofounder of the Group, Lee Strasberg, a name virtually synonymous with the American variant of the Stanislavsky system, 'method acting'. Many members of the original company of *The Crucible* also belonged to the Actor's Studio.

Most of the emphasis for *Death of a Salesman* in Part Two is on the two most significant productions: the original, directed by Kazan, opening 10 Feb. 1949 on Broadway, starring Cobb as Willy Loman, and the revival directed by Michael Rudman, opening 29 March 1984 on Broadway, starring Dustin Hoffman as Willy. Discussion will include CBS's television production of 15 Sept. 1985, directed by Volker Schlondorff but essentially the same as the New York production of the year before. To help illuminate interpretation, four others will at times be mentioned: the first London production, opening 28 July 1949, directed by Kazan and starring Paul Muni; the Circle in the Square (New York) performance, opening 26 June 1975, directed by George C. Scott who also played Willy;

1. Act I of Elia Kazan's Broadway production of *Death of a Salesman*, 1949. Lee J. Cobb (Willy Loman), Mildred Dunnock (Linda), Arthur Kennedy (Biff), Cameron Mitchell (Happy). Photograph © Eileen Darby.

2. Act I of Michael Rudman's Broadway production of *Death of a Salesman*, 1984. David Chandler (Bernard), Stephen Lang (Happy), Kate Reid (Linda), Dustin Hoffman (Willy Loman), John Malkovich (Biff), David Huddleston (Charley). Photograph © Inge Morath, by courtesy of Magnum Photos.

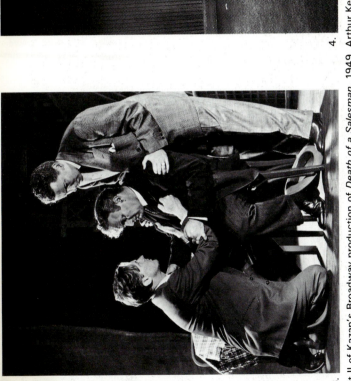

3. Act II of Kazan's Broadway production of *Death of a Salesman*, 1949. Arthur Kennedy (Biff), Lee J. Cobb (Willy Loman), Cameron Mitchell (Happy). Photograph © Eileen Darby.

4. Act II of Rudman's Broadway production of *Death of a Salesman*, 1984. Dustin Hoffman (Willy Loman). Photograph © Inge Morath, by courtesy of Magnum Photos.

5. Act I of Jed Harris's Broadway production of *The Crucible*, 1953. Fred Stewart (Reverend Parris), Arthur Kennedy (John Proctor), E.G. Marshall (Reverend Hale). Photograph by Alfredo Valente, © Billy Rose Theatre Collection.

6. Act IV of Bill Bryden's National Theatre production of *The Crucible*, transferred to the Comedy Theatre, 1981. Mark McManus (John Proctor), Lynn Farleigh (Elizabeth Proctor). Photograph © Michael Mayhew.

Michael Rudman's National Theatre presentation, opening 20 Sept. 1979 at the Lyttleton Theatre, featuring Warren Mitchell; and the Arthur Miller production in Beijing, China, opening 7 May 1983, starring Ying Ruocheng, who also translated the play.

Most of the emphasis for *The Crucible* is on three productions: the original, directed by Jed Harris, opening on Broadway 22 Jan. 1953; Laurence Olivier's for the National Theatre, opening at the Old Vic 19 Jan. 1965 and Bill Bryden's National Theatre production, opening 30 Oct. 1980 at the Cottesloe Theatre, transferring to the West End with some cast changes on 3 March 1981. To help illuminate interpretation, some references will be made to four others: the first in England, directed by Warren Jenkins, opening 9 Nov. 1954 at the Theatre Royal, Bristol; the first London presentation, directed by George Devine and Tony Richardson, opening at the Royal Court Theatre on 9 April 1956; John Berry's production for the Repertory Theatre of Lincoln Center, opening at the Vivienne Beaumont Theatre on 27 April 1972 and Barry Kyle and Nick Hamm's for the Royal Shakespeare Company/Nat West Tour in December 1984.

I have seen the New York productions of *Death of a Salesman* (on stage and television) and *The Crucible* just mentioned, as well as other American performances, but none outside the United States. I cite this as fact, not failing or boast. I rely on my memory only insofar as records of the productions have acted as reduced cues.

DEATH OF A SALESMAN

The impact of the original New York production was enormous. Reviewers called it 'great'; several noted that the audience wept during its course and remained after the final curtain call. When it opened in London five months later, critics were appreciative but moderate. In contrast to New York, said T. C. Worsley, London first-nighters failed to snuffle (*New Statesman and Nation*, 6 Aug. 1949). Reviewers tended to attribute the different responses to American and English national characteristics. When the play opened in

Paris in 1950, it created little stir; to the French, said Miller, 'Willy was a man from Mars'. In 1965, however, it was a major success there; by then, Frenchmen were 'up to their necks in time payments, broken washing machines, dreams of fantastic success, new apartment houses shading out the vegetables in the backyard, and the chromed anxiety of a society where nothing deserves existence that doesn't pay' ('What Makes Plays Endure?'). In 1979, responses in London also differed. Partly, as Barry Took noted, 'Thirty years on we stand where Willy Loman stood' (*Punch*, 3 Oct. 1979). Mostly, however, critics perceived the work as 'less a play about the American dream and more a drama about universal emptiness' (Milton Shulman, *Evening Standard*, 21 Sept. 1979). Benedict Nightingale spoke not of the play's American subjects but of its universal qualities, such as 'being old, frightened, aghast at failures behind and emptinesses ahead', 'the parent who seeks vicarious fulfilment in his children, and the child painfully trying to cohere his brainwashed remnants into a personality truly his own', and particularly 'the life-lies in which most of us sometimes find sanity and cause for survival' (*New Statesman*, 28 Sept. 1979). In its New York reemergence five years later, its impact remained – to the surprise of many, including Frank Rich (*New York Times*, 30 March 1984): 'We know its flaws by heart – the big secret withheld from the audience until Act II, and the symbolic old brother Ben . . . forever championing the American dream in literary prose. Yet how small and academic these quibbles look when set against the fact of the thunderous thing itself.'

15   DIRECTION

When Elia Kazan directed *Death of a Salesman* in 1949, after such acclaimed stagings as Tennessee Williams's *A Streetcar Named Desire* two years earlier, many considered him one of America's best directors. His name almost guaranteed a thrilling production that united convincing action, appropriate scenery, vivid groupings and striking movement. Describing

Death of a Salesman as his greatest achievement, reviews call his direction of it memorable, dynamic, powerful, vigorous and masterful. Harold Clurman cited the production as 'an example of real theatre: meaning and means unified by fine purpose' (*New Republic*, 28 Feb. 1949).

Kazan's interpretation focused on Willy himself, with all of Willy's contradictions. As noted in his production book, and as reviews confirm, compassion for Willy and fear of what the title says will happen to him were among the goals towards which dramatic means led. With Willy as the object of pity, society was what Kazan called 'the "heavy"'. Since Willy has adopted its values, he is a mass of contradictions, which Kazan brought out. Full of love and longing for success, needing affection and admiration, feeling himself a failure but worthy of success, compensating for a sense of worthlessness with a confident line of blarney, torn between a need to believe he is vital to the firm in New England and a knowledge that he is not, building his life and sense of esteem on the opinion of others but also trying to become preeminent and besting others, hating and loving the same people (thus considering them his enemies if they disapprove of anything he does, however minor, and his friends if they admire him), competing with his neighbour while acting friendly towards him, Willy is filled with anxiety. In production notes and in production, he exists in a world that tears him apart by competition and love. To him, suicide combines both: he can better everyone and win more of Biff's love by giving him 20 000 dollars. Suicide would demonstrate his control of his life, his ability to defeat the world that defeated him. Willy's ideal is to be not a little man but prominent, which is what he teaches his sons: win by personality, win by jungle strength, emerge on top. For Willy to accept the job Charley offers would be humiliating, since his nextdoor neighbour began where he did.

For Willy to face reality, as Biff proposes, would destroy him, Kazan notes (and theatricalises on stage), for it would invalidate his entire life. Thus, Willy flees from present to past – but into a past that exists only in his present mind. As Kazan recognises, the play has no flashbacks. Figures and incidents in Willy's mind are distorted by his fears and desires.

In his hallucinations, which Kazan calls daydreams, Willy attacks people against whom he failed to defend himself in real life; his memory and need romanticise Ben and Biff, who exist not as they were but as Willy sees them in his imagination (Ben absorbed with big deals, Biff confident and handsome, fawned upon by his comrades); Charley appears as Willy needs him to appear (ignorant, careless, ambitionless); in contrast to Linda as she exists in the present (a tough woman), she is dumb, loyal, patient, innocent, always available for sympathy. A characteristic of Kazan's technique is dynamism. Characters are active, not passive. In part, he achieves his results through one of the basics of the Stanislavsky system, emphasis on actors' underlying objectives (goals, or actions as they are sometimes called) as opposed to feelings. His directing notebook stresses the need to discover not merely what Willy feels but what he does, even in his daydreams. Instead of emphasising, for example, Willy's feeling of despair or helplessness, which is passive, he underscores a desire to compensate for such a feeling by urging the actor to attack, insult, condemn. Miller's text justifies Kazan's interpretation. Frustrated or even desperate that he may have wasted his life, Willy articulates the subtext: 'Ben, am I right? Don't you think I'm right?' The reiterated question makes clear the advice he seeks from the Ben of his imagination.

Another characteristic of Kazan is the creation of ensemble acting – in a context of Broadway production, where actors may not have met each other before the first rehearsal, where their backgrounds may be entirely different, where their training (if they had any) may have varied radically. Another repeated assessment of his *Death of a Salesman* is its ensemble acting, its lifelike give-and-take, its lack of a demarcation between pretence and conviction. Not only was truthfulness observed in the performances of the leading actors, it was also noted in those who had small roles, including Tom Pedi as the waiter and Hope Cameron as Letta. Harold Clurman called Pedi 'as real and tasty as a garlic salad', Cameron suggestive of 'a remarkably touching naïveté' (*New Republic*, 28 Feb. 1949). In a tribute to Kazan ('The *Salesman* Has a Birthday'), Miller records the director's 'marvelous wiles' that tripped 'the latches of the secret little doors that lead into the always different personalities of each actor. . . . He does not "direct", he creates a centre point, and then goes to each actor and creates the desire to move toward it. And they all meet, but for different reasons, and seem to have arrived there by themselves'.

Fortunately, Kazan has permitted the publication of an annotated scene in his production book, which analyses motivation, delivery of dialogue and business that directorially vivifies the text. Although production books do not record performance but express what the director aspires towards, Kazan's production fulfilled these aspirations.

While Bernard waits outside his father's office, he is dressed smoothly and seems to be 'a Big Man' (i.e. size conveys stature). Willy's voice, from the wings, reveals how he seems to the world. The two men have not seen each other for years, and when they did their relationship differed. Now they examine each other, noticing changes and wondering what has happened. Both, says Kazan, loved Biff. Behind his mask, Bernard tries to help, for he too has been curious as to what happened to his boyhood friend; this effort, which Willy appreciates, makes him feel guilty. Willy's banter with the secretary is how he thinks a salesman should behave with a girl. He picks up Bernard's tennis rackets, guiltily puts them down when Bernard calls him 'Uncle Willy', then recovers from the shock, since he does not want Bernard to see him the way he is and since Bernard is obviously successful (Willy wonders how and why). When Bernard tells Willy he must leave for Washington in a few minutes, he looks at his watch with a gesture similar to the one Ben used – a visually subtle connection of two successful men. To Willy, though Bernard tries to put him at ease, Bernard has become an affront, a source of humiliation. His very cigarette case seems a mystery to Willy. Naively asking the young man whether he will play tennis in Washington, Willy regards a private tennis court with awe and he wonders (as Kazan notes), 'How did the little schmuck do it?' When the subject turns to Biff, both try to determine what happened. As Willy invents transparent lies about Biff's success, Bernard plays with his Phi Beta Kappa key, his glasses and his watch. Although they apparently talk about Bernard's family and Biff's job, they are really examining each other (the subtext). At the news that Bernard has two sons, Willy is wounded, for he would like grandsons. Asked whether he is still with the same firm, Willy changes the subject, for he cannot tolerate the reality of his failure and Bernard's success; and Bernard, concealing his knowledge that Willy is a pathetic liar, averts his gaze out of embarrassment for the man.

Unable to conceal from himself the unreality of what he says, Willy breaks off his sputtering statements about Biff's accomplishments to ask why his son never became successful. Trying to speak and about to cry, he cannot talk. After he utters Bernard's name, he tenses in his chair and turns away from him. Full of pity, Bernard tries to help. Willy must force out his question as to why Biff failed, for he thinks there is a secret formula to success, a piece of advice he failed to give; and, head bowed, he cannot look at Bernard while asking. Gently, still trying to help Willy, Bernard says he does not know; unable to look directly at Willy, he sits on the desk with his head bowed, avoiding the cruelty of telling Willy the truth. Willy must plead, suddenly becoming direct, for he craves liberation from the hell of his guilt.

The preceding two paragraphs, drawn from Kazan's directing notes, demonstrate the meticulous care taken by this great director to uncover the psychological truths, human behaviour and social attitudes that underlie every detail of a play. In practice, they result in rich theatricalisations of a drama's inner and outer lives and help to set forth the basis of realistic ensemble acting.

By contrast, ensemble acting was missing from Michael Rudman's Broadway production. Eileen Blumenthal mentioned the 'lack of unity on stage, as if each actor's inner truth, rather than ensemble effort, were the ultimate goal' (*Village Voice*, 10 April 1984). Rudman's direction, said John Simon, ranged 'from uninventive to pedestrian; and the acting is uneven' (*New York*, 9 April 1984). The Woman in Boston was clearly too young (under 35, with a platinum blonde hairstyle suggestive of Jean Harlow), and one tended to shrug off her eviction from the hotel room as suitable. Both *Variety* and the *Times* noted the 'jarringly melodramatic' quality of Willy's boss, directed to be played 'as a snarling heavy' (Humm,

4 April 1984; Holly Hill, 3 April 1984). The absence of directorial unity was particularly evident in the company's different accents. In contrast to Kazan's, in which everyone sounded like a New Yorker, Rudman's did not. Dustin Hoffman and Stephen Lang had fine New York accents, but Kate Reid sounded as though she were from a different part of the country, let alone the same family (though she did not reveal her native Canadian accent), and John Huddleston seemed to live much farther away than next door. Perhaps John Malkovich aimed, through speech, to suggest someone who had lived away from New York for many years and who reverted to his original accent in moments of stress, for in the restaurant scene it emerged.

Such deficiencies aside, Rudman's production had several virtues, notably a focus different from (and as valid as) Kazan's. Its emphasis was not a man destroyed by false values but 'the inextricable love and hate that bind Willy and his older son' (Allan Wallach, *Newsday*, 30 March 1984). Here, as Frank Rich states, 'It's not Willy's pointless death that moves us; it's Biff's decision to go on living' (*New York Times*, 30 March 1984). In his own way, Rudman achieved extraordinarily realistic effects, sometimes through overlapping dialogue. For instance, the text has:

WILLY: Biff is a lazy bum!
LINDA: They're sleeping. Get something to eat. Go on down.

In performance (and I draw this detail from the television version):

WILLY: (*shouting*) Biff is a lazy –
LINDA: (*hushing him as she interrupts*) They're sleeping.
WILLY: (*whispering*) – bum!
LINDA: (*gently, pleading with him*) Get something to eat. Go on down.

Whereas elation marked the conclusion of both Kazan's and Rudman's productions, which stressed the possibility of hope throughout, George C. Scott's enveloped the audience, as Douglas Watt says, 'in an atmosphere of defeat' and its 'uneven direction' made it less gripping than it otherwise might have been (*Daily News*, 27 June 1975). Numerous reviewers commented on the colour-blind casting of the neighbours, played by Black actors, as a mistaken directorial choice, possibly to make more plausible Willy's refusal of a job offer from Charley (which Miller makes plausible enough), but as they observed, if Willy would not work for a Black neighbour he would not (in 1949) live next door to one, he would not turn to one for financial help and he would not employ a nonracial slur like 'anemic' for the son. For no reason that I or any reviewer could make out, Scott made two characters of the Woman in Boston.

In Miller's Beijing production, the connecting thread was everyone's love for Willy. Not that they necessarily admired him, indeed they often could not stand him, but they were drawn to his lack of cynicism and the intensity of his belief, commitment and love. As Miller explained to the actor playing Charley, the character greatly admires Linda and envies 'Willy's imagination, the condiments with which he sprinkles his life as contrasted with the blandness of Charley's more rational existence. Charley can laugh at Willy as a fool, but he is never bored by him'. Instead of aiming to make the Lomans Chinese in China or Americans in America, Miller directed the actors not to act like Americans (in which case they would imitate American movies, which would result in a performance twice removed from reality), but to make the play Chinese, albeit in a Lomanlike American situation. The result, he claims, was 'something akin to American body movements' by 'the Lomans-as-Chinese-looking people . . . in some country of the mind, I suppose, certainly not in any earthly geography'. To the actor who played Ben, he explained that the character is not a ghost (which a Chinese play might contain) but one who, though dead, exists in Willy's memory, endowed with qualities that are not necessarily realistic. He added: 'We all remember actual people we once knew but we remember them in a nonobjective way that emphasises and even parodies some of their qualities'. Since the actors did not know how to play casino, Willy and Charley played gin rummy, building to a point where Willy, instead of calling a build his own, claims an ace. When the actresses playing Miss Forsythe and the Woman in Boston wanted to know whether their characters were bad women or prostitutes, Miller to avoid stereotypes suggested to the former that she was what she said she was, a photographer's model now having a rest and drink after a hard day's work and that only Happy, who need not be believed, denigrates her; and to the latter, that she was a lonely woman who genuinely likes Willy and the way he talks, sees him for dinner a few times a month and talks and acts with him as if they were married for a night. 'It would have been difficult to add', says Miller, 'that she might have had a similar relation to a couple of other salesmen from time to time and still not be thought of as a prostitute or even Bad. But this would also be hard to explain in parts of the United States'. What was important in both cases was that the actresses should not behave like prostitutes or vamps. One scene prompted him to reexamine his text on the basis of what he had written, not what he remembered. The Chinese Woman in Boston behaved in a baroque fashion towards Willy, circling him as if in a dream, offering him a drink with outstretched arms and with a long white silk shawl flowing over her back. The 'poetic fantasy' of her movements proved so intriguing that Miller returned to the dialogue, where he found, to his surprise, that he 'had originally intended an hallucinatory surrealism which had somehow gotten lost in the various productions, including the original'. Instead of talking to each other realistically, a manner directors had imposed on the sequence, they talked past each other, stating 'dreamlike, disjointed, and intensively compressed positions'. He therefore changed his directorial approach towards one that emphasised uncommunicative dislocation despite physical connection.

What the interpretations of Miss Forsythe and the Woman in Boston suggest, as do some of Kazan's commentaries, is the need to ground actors in belief in specific qualities – regardless of whether spectators become aware of the precise details. What matters is that the actors understand them and use them as a basis on which to build credibility.

16   SCENERY AND LIGHTING

Jo Mielziner, who designed the original setting and lighting for *Death of a Salesman*, discloses that only a small portion of a stage designer's work is creative – the exercise of his imagination to determine the visual embodiment of the author's text – and that about 85 per cent of his time is spent making sure that what he has imagined and designed is properly executed. With *Death of a Salesman*, Mielziner's 15 per cent was so imaginative and appropriate for the play's artistic and practical requirements that Miller not only incorporated the design into the published text, it also set the model for many productions that followed. As originally written, says Mielziner, Miller described such scenic elements as the house once surrounded by trees and open sky but now hemmed in by apartment houses, but after 40-odd scenes that he did not integrate visually, he concluded: 'The scenic solution to this production will have to be an imaginative and simple one. I don't know the answer, but the designer must work out something which makes the script flow easily'. Mielziner did so. A basic problem was not only that the play requires many different scenic locations but that it demands instantaneous change from present to past and back again. Furthermore, Mielziner had to make these transitions visually clear to the audience, which would otherwise find them confusing, and he felt he must do so without losing what he perceived to be the play's most important visual symbol and major background, the house. Therefore, he decided that the house itself should be the main setting, with all other scenes played on the forestage. Instead of blacking out the stage or lowering the curtain, he used a few easily moved properties and fluid lighting effects.

Because the set had to be practical (that is, capable of being used by the actors), various conundrums presented themselves. Perhaps the major problem was the transition that required Biff and Happy to vanish from their bedroom and reappear moments later on the stage floor, years younger and costumed differently. His solution of how to accomplish this without having the audience see the actors leave the bedroom was to build an inner frame in the beds that was also an elevator, have the 'pillows' made of papier-mâché with depressions that concealed the actors' heads, and stiffen the blankets to stay in place – thereby permitting the actors to be lowered without destroying the illusion that they were still in bed. The forestage had to be large enough to permit them to move where the director required them to move (the solution, to build it over part of the front row of seats, required a concession by the producer, who lost income from those seats). The number of properties were pared to permit apparently instantaneous scene changes (for instance, the same desk served both Howard's and Charley's offices). Initially, Mielziner designed a trick trapdoor that let a gravestone rise for the Requiem, but he and Kazan agreed to eliminate it partly because the audience's imagination would provide the cemetery setting and partly because if they used it people might be so busy wondering how the trick was done, they would miss the dialogue and mood.

The Boston hotel room employed a projection of cheap wallpaper instead of properties. Lighting was frequently used to create quick changes between present and imagined past. For example, on a backdrop of unbleached muslin, Mielziner had the apartment buildings, especially the windows, painted in transparent colours that would appear bright when lighted from behind. When the scene changed to hallucinatory time past, numerous projection units, like magic lanterns, threw leaf patterns on the backdrop and part of the Loman house from both auditorium and backstage, removing the oppressive structures and providing a sense of free outdoors in what Willy considered the springtime of his life.

Not only did Miller revise the play in order to incorporate the design plan, he also incorporates in the published text many practical solutions to scenic problems. For example, '*The apartment houses are fading out, and the entire house and surroundings become covered with leaves*'. While Linda talks to Biff on the telephone, Howard wheels onstage a small typewriter table on which is a wire recorder, and he plugs it in; as lights fade on her they rise on him. At the end of his scene: '*He starts to go, turns, remembering the recorder, starts to push off the table holding the recorder*'. A blackout concludes Willy's scene in

Charley's office, then a red glow appears behind a screen on the opposite side of the stage. A waiter appears, carrying a table, followed by Happy, who carries two chairs. As realistic motivation, Miller has the waiter say, 'That's all right, Mr. Loman. I can handle it myself' – whereupon he takes the chairs and sets them down.

Critics responded appreciatively to Mielziner's imaginative and functional set. In it, 'everything moves around easily between . . . dream world and reality' (*Time*, 21 Feb. 1949); in the 'ingenious skeletonised set . . . the Loman household is dwarfed and crushed under the weight of the stone and brick of the apartment buildings which have sprung up around it' (John Beaufort, *Christian Science Monitor*, 19 Feb. 1949). Miller has said that a major question posed by the play is how a man may make the outside world a home. However he might try, Mielziner's set shows the problem: an environment that enshadows it, threatening to crush it and permitting nothing to grow. Tensions between realistic set pieces (such as the refrigerator) and unrealistic outlines (such as the roof) mirror tensions between reality and daydreams. Furthermore, the disharmony between the setting the audience sees and the music it hears (a flute suggests grass, trees and horizon) reflects the contradictions and disharmonies within Willy's character. Only one assessment of Mielziner's set was negative (Lee Newton, *Daily Worker*, 14 Feb. 1949): 'Murky and sombre in appearance, it reflected nothing of the Salesman who had . . . bought it and worked on it for 25 years, putting a lot of himself into it. Such a house would have been brighter – the Salesman was a great one for a joke and a funny story – and would certainly have given more outward appearances of attempts to keep up with the Joneses'.

Ben Edwards's 1984 set so clearly derived from Mielziner's that, as Clive Barnes stated, it paid homage to it (*New York Post*, 30 March 1984). Marjorie Kellogg's set for Circle in the Square demonstrated not that the play belongs to a proscenium arch theatre (Douglas Watt, *Daily News*, 27 June 1975; Martin Gottfried, *New York Post*, 27 June 1975), but that this theatre's rectangular space, unwieldy for so many plays, was disastrous for this. Whereas Mielziner's set gave the appearance of simplicity, John Gunter's, for the National Theatre, seemed overstated. Whenever the action shifted from present to daydreamed past, said Michael Billington, the setting 'slides sleekly back' and 'a skycloth is laboriously unveiled at the rear of the stage'; for the funeral, 'the back-curtain rises to reveal a New York graveyard teaming with anonymous memorials'. This 'heavy-handed exaggeration' and 'sumptuous over-production' were better suited to a musical (*Guardian*, 22 Sept. 1979).

Because of the different dramatic medium, Tony Walton's design for television (1985) differed from Mielziner's concept. Walton added such details as worn furniture, paint peeling from window sills, a barely discernible cemetery in the far background. In Ben's scenes, a bright white background created atmosphere. At the start of the scene in Howard's office one could see a clear day through the windows (unfortunately, one could also see obviously painted office buildings); after Willy becomes desperate one could discern rain pouring on the outside window pane. Brighter colours and lighting were employed for the imagined scenes of time past (pinks, for instance, instead of browns for the backgrounds of the exterior) – reflecting a cheerier, happier view of life.

17 ACTING

Willy Loman   Lee J. Cobb, the first Willy Loman, is a large man, a 'walrus' as the published play describes him. Extremely realistic in conception and execution, his acting is also suggestive of immensity. His height, girth and full-bodied low baritone voice suggest epic dimensions. He has a stage presence that compels notice, and when Linda demands that attention be paid to him audiences agree, for they have already complied with her admonition. Recall Cobb's portrayal of the crooked union leader in Kazan's film *On the Waterfront*. How many other actors could convey such strength when pitted against an antagonist played by the young Marlon Brando? Despite the variety of his different portraits, Cobb – even as a salesman at the end of his rope – presents a titanic image. For a long while, this image dominated the casting of Willy in America: large or seemingly large men performed the role.

Calling his performance 'heroic', Brooks Atkinson noted its combination of 'familiar and folksy' details with 'something of the grand manner in the big size and the deep tone' (*New York Times*, 11 Feb. 1949). George Currie said that he 'would out-shout fate' (*Brooklyn Eagle*, 11 Feb. 1949). 'Mammoth' was the term used by Howard Barnes, who stated that in Cobb's hands Willy's frustrations and suicide become 'matters of tremendous import. With a vast range of gesture and diction, he gives Willy a curious stature in his downfall' (*New York Herald Tribune*, 11 Feb. 1949).

At least some of the discussion of *Death of a Salesman* as tragedy derives from Cobb's performance. To John Simon, 'Cobb was the tragedy' (*New York*, 9 April 1984). Insisting on the 'grandeur' that he conveyed, Brooks Atkinson said (*New York Times*, 20 Feb. 1949), 'He keeps it on the high plane of tragic acting – larger than the specific life it is describing. Willy is not a great man, but his tragedy is great, partly because of the power and range of Mr. Cobb's acting. When Willy's life collapses, a whole world crashes because Mr. Cobb fills the play with so much solid humanity. In terms of the business world Willy is insignificant. But in terms of life he is a hero'.

Much of Cobb's effectiveness lay in his combining stature with touches of reality. In Thomas R. Dash's words, 'It is a performance of superb shading' (*Women's Wear Daily*, 11 Feb. 1949). Robert Garland remarked on Cobb's ability to test one's patience and break one's heart, often at the same time (*New York Journal American*, 11 Feb. 1949). Eric Bentley called his acting 'a rock of a performance, strong enough to hold up any play' (*Theatre Arts*, Nov. 1949, revised in Hurrel: I quote from the original). And:

> Lee Cobb's work in this play is a most triumphant vindication of the Group [Theatre]'s method. He brings to the drama a knowledge of the salesman's character (as expressed in his limbs, the hunch of his shoulders, in vocal intonation, in facial expression) which is not provided in the script. What an idiom represents in language, Mr. Cobb can manifest in stance or vocal colour. Each small movement seems to come welling up from the weary,

wounded soul. According to plan, Mr. Cobb identifies himself with the role; and the audience identifies itself with Mr. Cobb.

In *Salesman in Beijing*, Miller describes Cobb's very laughter as 'sad and somehow filled with a bottomless kind of wanting for love, admiration, friendship'. When the actor says, in the same speech, that since life is short a few jokes are in order, that he jokes too much and is fat and foolish to look at, 'For Lee it was one of the moments when he reached a rarely achieved relaxation, a private calm that at the same time was filled with anxiety'. John Beaufort singled out a particularly fine moment in the performance, Cobb's fondling of Bernard's gold cigarette case, as 'a gesture of wistful admiration for the material success which has eluded all his hustling' (*Christian Science Monitor*, 19 Feb. 1949). In *Salesman in Beijing*, Miller says that Cobb invented this business: as Cobb with almost no confidence tries to inflate Biff's career, the successful Bernard offers him a cigarette, but instead of taking one Cobb absent-mindedly takes the case and continues to talk of Biff's big doings.

> And as he turns the gold case over in his hand, it silently embodies Bernard's success and his son's failure, and he then simply hands it back to Bernard. It seems so easy, but it is terribly hard to 'not-see' something one is looking at, and to 'not-think' what one is thinking, for the whole action is being done without the least deliberation, yet before our eyes. . . . I think it was Lee's masterstroke, a little thing that shone forth his greatness.

Like Lee J. Cobb, Dustin Hoffman was younger than Willy Loman – though he was older than Cobb was in 1949 (45 to Cobb's 37). Unlike Cobb, Hoffman was a major film actor when he undertook the role. In terms of the expense of producing a play on Broadway in 1984 and backers' fears that a nonmusical or noncomedy would not repay its investment, his decision to play Willy was as much the acquisition of a 'bankable' movie star as it was that of an excellent actor. The presence of the man who had portrayed the youth in *The Graduate*, the single father in *Kramer vs. Kramer*, and the convincing impersonator of a woman in *Tootsie* persuaded CBS to support the project to the sum of $850 000. Part of CBS's return was an option to produce the work, with

Hoffman, on television. Even so, the undertaking was risky. Hoffman agreed to draw a minimum salary of $735 per week until the play turned a profit, though after that he would receive a percentage of the gross receipts (*New York Times*, 8 March 1984). Happily for all, the production was successful.

Hoffman's casting represents a major break with American theatrical tradition in respect to the title role. Actually, Miller originally conceived of Willy as a small man. When Cobb was cast, he changed the description of Willy from 'shrimp' to 'walrus'; for Hoffman, it returned to 'shrimp'. He would not be a walrus, said Hoffman in an interview, he would be 'a spitfire' (*New York Times*, 8 March 1984). Instead of a bulky salesman, Hoffman was a little boat seeking a harbour, as Linda calls Willy in the text. Jack Kroll compares the actors: 'Lee J. Cobb's original, indelible Willy was a rumpled hulk; his body sagged like a fighter who's taken too many blows. Hoffman's Willy is dapper and drained; he's like a hoofer who can't buck and wing anymore' (*Newsweek*, 9 April 1984).

Whereas the large Cobb conveyed immense size and stature, the short, slim Hoffman imparted reduced size and stature. Whereas the bald Cobb wore a toupee (perhaps to suggest vanity, though no action called attention to it and he usually wore one in his motion picture roles anyway), Hoffman had his full head of hair shaved to near baldness so that he might convincingly wear a thinning, silvery hairpiece. He made up to look sallow and sunken-cheeked, and he had slightly oversized, rimless eyeglasses to emphasise facial smallness. To communicate visually what the text suggests, that he is starving himself to death, his clothes were a size too large. For age, he lowered his baritone voice to almost a rasp (a backstage visitor, solicitous of his health, inquired about his cold, to be informed by Hoffman in clear, higher tones than the character had, that he was perfectly fine and had changed his voice to suit the role). Initially, he patterned his voice on his father's, his accent on Miller's; eventually, both models fused with a Willy of his invention.

But Hoffman did more than recreate external details. This extraordinary actor worked from within as well as without. His cracked voice suggested a man on the verge of breaking. His whining qualities early in the play made his fury when

Howard rejects him all the more devastating. When in a last plea for dignity he tells Howard that one cannot eat an orange and discard the peel, he seemed to embody a decaying peel. As Dan Isaac writes, 'It is with this moment that playwright Miller perfectly synthesised his social message with the self-destruct tendencies of his protagonist. And Hoffman takes this scene and turns it into a devastating heartrending occasion. It is here that the American salesman, filled with dreams for an ever-productive future, turns into an aging useless Everyman' (*Chelsea Clinton News*, 19 April 1984). John Beaufort calls the performance 'a revelation. The actor preserves Willy's facade so resolutely and with so few outward signs of cracking that the breakdowns, when they do occur, are the more devastating' (*Christian Science Monitor*, 30 March 1984).

Like Cobb a realistic actor, Hoffman is unlike Cobb in that he works on a smaller scale. Whereas Cobb seemed larger than life, Hoffman seems entirely proportionate. Whereas Cobb's persona and performance contrasted ironically with the 'low man' status suggested by Willy's surname, Hoffman's conformed to it. Whereas Cobb conveyed a heightened Everyman, Hoffman seemed not a lowered but simply an unheightened everyone, with an appropriately lower-case initial letter. As Frank Rich perceives, when Willy denies Biff's assertion that he is 'a dime a dozen', Hoffman's rants make him appear so small 'that we fear the price quoted by Biff may, if anything, be too high'. His 'bouncy final exit' is not the death of a tragic hero but that of a salesman, who 'rides to suicide, as he rode through life, on the foolish, empty pride of "a smile and a shoeshine"' (*New York Times*, 30 March 1984). Deliberately, he played an individual human being, not an abstract genre. The result, pace Rich, was an almost inadvertently tragic figure. When Linda demands that attention be paid, we respond sympathetically, recognising that this demand must be made of such a man before one would do so. Both Cobb and Hoffman gave monumental performances, but while Cobb evoked a towering figure to whom monuments are built, Hoffman portrayed a puny figure to whom one would not consider building a monument until urged to do so. Hoffman's performance had 'the demonic ferocity that is his glory as an actor' (Richard Schickel, *Time*, 9 April 1984).

Hoffman enters so deeply into the character of Willy that even when he follows Miller's stage directions his conviction gives the impression that his actions are his own invention. At the start of the play, for example, Miller directs him to cross the stage carrying his sample cases. Since '*his exhaustion is apparent*', once he unlocks the door and enters the kitchen he '*thankfully lets his burden down, feeling the soreness of his palms. A word-sigh escapes his lips – it might be* "Oh, boy, oh, boy."' Hoffman followed these directions to the very letter. His utter exhaustion, magnified by his isolation within the cavernous setting (intensified by the lighting and the seemingly immense suitcases), created a poignance that seemed refreshingly new, for it was an act of artistic creation so fully realised that had one not been familiar with the play and cast list one might wonder how long after this tired old man appeared the popular movie star would enter. Hoffman fills literally hundreds of stage moments with credibility derived in part from sensitive reading of the text and in part from his great histrionic skill in conveying the meaning of these moments as part of a character design. Frank Rich observes that when Willy remembers his father's departure while he was a child and says he still feels sort of temporary about himself, 'As Mr. Hoffman's voice breaks on the word "temporary", his spirit cracks into defeat. From then on, it's a merciless drop to the bottom of his "strange thoughts" – the hallucinatory memory sequences that send him careening in and out of a lifetime of anxiety' (*New York Times*, 30 March 1984). More so than Cobb, who suggested defiance of fate, Hoffman emphasises Willy's insecurity. At the end of the first act, Linda twice interrupts him when he gives Biff advice. In the text, he first demands she let him finish what he has been trying to say, then resumes his advice; next, he shouts her down, then continues advising his son. In performance, Hoffman first slapped her on the knee to emphasise his irritation at her interruption; when he did so a second time, he added a gentle pat on her shoulder, conveying an annoyance with himself for having treated her that way, especially before their children. In the restaurant scene, a stage direction has Willy nod affirmatively when he asks Biff what happened and whether his visit to Oliver went satisfactorily. In performance, Hoffman –

aching for good news from his son – pats Biff's hair while he nods and asks his question. When he pleads with Howard to take him off the road, 'his initial tentativeness gives way to the cracked voice of a man veering out of control' (Allan Wallach, *Newsday*, 30 March 1984).

Hoffman's performance is all the more heartbreaking because of the comic moments he creates. While he and Charley play casino, for instance, he points out the ceiling he had put up in the living room; as Charley glances at it, Hoffman sneaks a look at the cards in Charley's hand. To clink a toast, he takes Biff's glass (while Biff holds it) as well as his own. I have described the Kazan–Cobb interpretation of the scene between Willy and grown-up Bernard. Although Hoffman does not employ the business with the cigarette case invented by Cobb, he endows the scene with considerable vitality and insight of his own. As described by Edwin Wilson: 'In quick succession, he goes through a series of contrasting emotions. One moment he is faking a casual air; the next he is swallowing his pride to congratulate Bernard, and the next he is trying desperately to convince himself that his own boys will be just as successful' (*Wall Street Journal*, 4 April 1984). Brendan Gill's insight is pertinent: 'From time to time, [Hoffman's] Willy catches sight of himself and drolly takes his measure; he is not so much blind to the person he has become as lacking any means of accommodating to that person' (*New Yorker*, 9 April 1984). Although Hoffman's Willy has wrong dreams about becoming a success, he focuses on the love of his older son. Thus, when he goes to his car (and to death), he virtually dances with glee, imagining how much the young man will enjoy the gift of $20 000.

Hoffman carefully shows Willy's contradictions – the sales-man's smile that conceals his unhappiness, the playful moments of dancing and placing a hand on one of his wife's breasts before giving way to impotent anger, the tensions revealed by how he sits on a chair before a momentary pleasure relaxes his body and his face breaks out in a smile. Not only does Hoffman revel in these explosively sudden contradictions, he finds ways to reveal the past in the present. Benedict Nightingale astutely observes (*New York Times*, 8 April 1984):

You can very clearly see the not-unsuccessful hustler he was years ago: flirting with the secretaries, swapping risqué jokes with the buyers, talking more than enough to make a sale and getting a reputation as a loudmouth in the process. To suggest what a character was, while simultaneously showing what he has become, is one of the more interesting feats open to an actor; and Mr. Hoffman achieves it, even when the script isn't giving him direct access to the past.

Thirty-five years earlier, Books Atkinson described Cobb's Willy: 'the spring has gone from his step, the smile from his face and the heartiness from his personality' (*New York Times*, 11 Feb. 1949). Hoffman takes a different route. In desperation, the spring, smile and heartiness remain, almost ghosts of their former selves, occasionally energised into life. When he leaves Linda to see Howard and then his sons, he is so happy, he joyfully dances with her before his exit. Before leaving to kill himself, he is so pleased at what his death will accomplish, he shakes his behind, as if ready for a turn on the dance floor.

Hoffman has rethought the thrust of the role and its physical characteristics; reexamining each moment, he has filtered it through his distinctive actor sensibilities. The final reunion of Willy and Biff, for example, was tremendously moving when enacted by Cobb: 'There is a moment when Cobb almost flings [Arthur] Kennedy to the audience, then draws him back in a flood of fatherly love. I defy anyone to escape the power of that moment' (Whitney Bolton, *Morning Telegraph*, 12 Feb. 1949). Though entirely different, Hoffman's enactment is just as moving and powerful. When Biff embraces and kisses Willy in this climactic scene, Hoffman returns neither embrace nor kiss – not because he lacks love but because after seventeen years he is unaccustomed to this experience. He flaps his arms about as though he wants to return both embrace and kiss, but he is so unprepared to receive either, he almost fears to touch his son lest he be rejected again. His happiness is very real, but his astonishment overwhelms him and overcomes his ability to return openly such affection.

As indicated, Hoffman's performance develops from careful attention to external details and from equally precise investigation of emotional truth. In a different binary statement of his achievement, Holly Hill perceives (*Times*, 3 April 1984):

'He plays him from the inside out in the American naturalistic tradition, but also comments on the character from a distance, taking perhaps not a leaf but a scrap from [Bertolt] Brecht. We cannot help but sense his personal love for the character in addition to his judgement of Willy as victim of his own evasions as well as of false values'.

By contrast, Paul Muni's performance appears to have been chiefly a matter of externals. In *Salesman in Beijing*, Miller states that Muni 'played the "type", going so far as to record the entire role on a gigantic reel of tape under his wife's tutelage and then imitate himself in a rendition of the "American Salesman", with the wooden smile and the "glad hand"'. As Miller told Ronald Hayman, Muni had reached a stage in his career 'when he was listening to his own voice – he was a very good actor but his style had been superseded twenty years earlier really. The style was too studied, too technical. There was too little real inner life in his performance'.

Also by contrast (with both Cobb and Hoffman), George C. Scott played Willy with the goal (as I infer from his performance) of creating a character as different as possible from the one he performed in the film *The Hospital*. His Willy had so little warmth, it was impossible to imagine why his sons ever adored him or his wife loved him. The performance seemed a conglomeration of solely external details. With a bald wig, a baggy suit, his usual raspy voice, a fixed and ghastly idiot-like grin, a delivery that verged upon rant, and a hint that a mild shove might move the character towards insanity, Scott did not so much convey Willy as he did an actor on stage playing Willy. In the words of one reviewer (Christopher Sharp, *Women's Wear Daily*, 27 June 1975):

> Willy Loman no longer comes off as a typical loser being stampeded in the American rat race. George C. Scott's gnome-like Loman is such a distinct individual that there is no mistaking him for a universal failure. Scott's Loman is the exception rather than the rule. Loman is portrayed by Miller as a loser because he is a victim of a social disease: He is consumed by the American drive to find success. In this version, Loman is so bizarre that it seems he has only himself to blame for his crackup. We come away from this evening thinking that society is OK; it is only Willy Loman who is in the wrong.

Whereas Cobb created a tradition in America as an over-sized Willy, Muni created one in England of a small Willy crushed by larger social forces – 'Wee Willy Loman', as Ivor Brown called him (*Observer*, 31 July 1949). Warren Mitchell is in that tradition. As John Elsom says, his Willy 'is obviously somebody who, even in his younger days and with the best PR in the world, could never seem to be anything other than a second-rate hustler' (*Listener*, 27 Sept. 1979). At variance with the text, he appeared as an 'untidy little man' wearing a 'shabby suit' (B. A. Young, *Financial Times*, 21 Sept. 1979). To at least two reviewers, his Willy suggested (as both said) 'a cornered rat' (Peter Jenkins, *Spectator*, 29 Sept. 1979; Peter Lewis, *Daily Mail*, 21 Sept. 1979), with what the latter called 'the philosophy of a toady'. Such a person lacks even nontragic stature.

According to Miller (*Salesman in Beijing*), Ying Ruocheng is 'about the size and shape of [James] Cagney, balanced on short legs, a compact man who is able to come on cold, step onto the forestage and simply call up the feelings and joys of his great moment, decades ago, when through Biff he felt he was within inches of some fabled victory over life's ignominious leveling'. Ying sees Willy 'as a little bantam with quick fists and the irreducible demand that life give him its meaning and significance and honour'. To Ying, Willy was very Chinese, in that 'we're always . . . finding some hope where there really isn't any. It's our whole history'. For Willy's final moments, before he leaves to commit suicide, Ying used an image to overcome a slumping attitude: 'Actually, you know – when a suicide looks through his noose he sees the most beautiful landscape, a serene place of long vistas and pools of water and lovely trees, and he is going toward that'.

Biff Anyone familiar with Arthur Kennedy's film per-formances – such as the younger brother in *City for Conquest* and *Champion*, the young father in *The Window* – can imagine the blend of sincerity and intensity he brought to the role of Biff in 1949. Reviewers commented appreciatively on his turbulent and forceful performance, his ability to capture the character's passion, disillusionment and frustration.

Unlike John Malkovich, who was Biff in 1984 and who looked younger than the character's 34 years, Kennedy looked the same age (actually, he was a year older). With what seemed to be a hairpiece (still less effective on television than on stage), Malkovich looked, more than Kennedy, like a conventional leading man. Furthermore, it was easier to believe that Kennedy used to be a football player than that Malkovich did. Whereas Kennedy was very much of the late 1940s in his acting style, conveying a young man's inner turbulence, Malkovich was very much of the mid-1980s in his: flat-toned, nasal, with minimally inflected speech and a casual-cool manner.

Anger and drive to make his father face the truth seemed to dominate Kennedy's scenes with Willy in Act II. If Miller did not add stage directions to Biff's final scene with Willy to convey what Kennedy did, then Kennedy managed to embody what these directions urged him to do. Although the dialogue would not suggest anger or a battle, this became the texture of their final confrontation, giving theatrical impact to Biff's determination. When he tells his father that he himself is not a leader of men, '*In his fury, Biff*' – or Kennedy – '*seems on the verge of attacking his father*'. After calling him vengeful and spiteful, Willy starts up the stairs, frightened that his son might hurt him. Indeed, Biff grabs him and as he calls himself a nothing, Biff-Kennedy is '*at the peak of his fury*', which is then spent and he collapses in his father's arms. Malkovich was less furious than he was in a state of unhappy, frantic desperation, for he seemed to aim to save both of their lives.

As the anonymous reviewer of *Variety* noted, Malkovich played Biff 'not as an angry victim seeking revenge on a wrongheaded parent, but as a wounded and confused man striving for peace through truth' (4 April 1984). Unlike Kennedy, he stressed Biff's vulnerability. As he said in an interview (*New York Times*, 31 March 1984), Biff 'needs Willy's blessing. For him, that's what the play's about'. One of his more riveting moments occurred during the restaurant scene, when his angry plea screamed at his brother, 'Help him!', dissolved into tears as he literally cried, 'Help me!' Particularly commendable, his 'anguished puzzlement never gives way to self-pity' (*Time*, 9 April 1984).

In Beijing, Biff emerged as a highly ironic character. Instead of venting self-pity when he tells his brother that while he has tried not to waste his life he has done nothing but waste it, the actor gave the speech with a lightly self-mocking grin, then tossed his old football helmet back into the chest beside the bed, from which he had picked it up, and walked away. When Biff promises his mother he will remain in New York to apply himself in business, Miller urged the actor to work against the stereotype of repentant son with noble resolution: 'You shouldn't have any emotion at all here. Except maybe that your trip back to the ranch is being interrupted'.

Happy   Although reviewers praised Cameron Mitchell's braggadoccio as Happy in the original production, Harold Clurman had an apt reservation: the actor was 'eminently likable, but for the play's thesis he ought also to be something of a comic stinker' (in Weales, *Salesman*). Insufficient critical acclaim has been given to Stephen Lang, whose Happy in 1984 is the best I have seen. Lang's technical proficiency (just as Happy is truly Willy's son, his values being those of his father, Lang had the same New York accent as Hoffman) was the start, not finish, of a superlative performance. After moments, one understands not only why he is a lady's man but also why only a simple woman would be taken in by him. When Lang asked, rhetorically, whether his habit of seducing the fiancées of executives was not truly 'a crummy characteristic', he seemed immensely pleased with himself as he showed off for his older brother. While telling Biff that he too longs for a woman of substance, he focused on himself in a mirror, preening, brilliantly conveying the character's insincerity. When Happy leaves his father in the lurch in the restaurant and persuades his brother to do the same, Lang conveyed the younger son's revenge on a father who preferred the older. As Holly Hill observes in one of the few appreciations of his performance, he never calls attention to the fact that he is acting (*Times*, 3 April 1984).

Linda   Most critics called Mildred Dunnock unforgettable.

With heartbreaking simplicity, sincerity and restraint, realising 'a characterisation beautiful in its drabness' (Robert Coleman, *Daily Mirror*, 11 Feb. 1949), she was 'a symbolic beacon of everything sound in the production' (Harold Clurman, *New Republic*, 28 Feb. 1949). Whereas Kazan cast a small, frail-looking woman to contrast with a mountainous Willy, Rudman cast a large, powerful-looking woman to contrast with a small Willy. Like Dunnock in 1949, Kate Reid in 1984 became the foundation and support of the family. Her performance contained wonderful moments, such as removing Willy's glasses in order to snuggle in his arms in bed in Act I. Still, as Holly Hill states, 'She is excellent as the strength of the family – when she says "pay attention" you had better stand to – but she attempts little more, not even the period Brooklyn accents displayed so well by the rest of her family' – or at least by Willy and Happy. While Reid does not whine, 'hers is an adequate performance' (*Times*, 3 April 1984).

In Beijing, Zhu Lin dealt with Willy as if 'always reaching a hand out as to a child who cannot walk without falling down'. Early in rehearsals, she indulged a tendency – a latent danger in the role – towards tearful sentimentality, reminding Miller of actresses who had played Jewish mothers in the Yiddish theatre and Irish mothers in movies of the 1930s – like this Chinese mother 'a lachrymose fount'. Gradually, however, Zhu abandoned sentimental devices that draw sympathy from audiences, realising instead that Linda has pressing objectives in relationship to other characters: for instance, to persuade Biff to find a job in New York. She realised too that, as Miller says, Linda is 'the woman on whom Willy relies, rather than the type to mop up after him'. By performance time, she became the kind of woman 'who is strong by concealing her strength'. She suppressed all hint of tears until her final words, that they are free, 'and even there she seemed to thread an irony through her anguish'. Particularly important to Zhu was Miller's explanation that Linda and Willy are still physically in love (in the traditional Group Theatre manner, Miller gave the actress a biography: Linda's family disapproved of Willy because he lacked money and prospects, and she in effect ran off with him). While Miller may not have known this aspect, his explanation that physical love remained between the Loman parents helped the actress to understand Linda as a Western woman. (As Elizabeth Wichmann, an American expert in Beijing opera who has performed in China, and her husband Liu Dan, a Chinese artist now working in America, told me, the fundamental family relationship in China is between parent and child, but in contemporary America it is between husband and wife, whose sexual affinity continues to be an important element despite their age. While the Chinese view of American women as highly charged sexually may reflect an official attitude of the time, it is a view that could help a performer interpret a character of a different culture.) Zhu's understanding of Linda manifested itself not only in her scenes with Willy, but also in the important opening moments of the play, where she demonstrates sincere alarm at Willy's unexpected return home.

THE CRUCIBLE

When *The Crucible* opened on Broadway in 1953, most reviewers received it with respectful praise. A few went further, for instance: 'a play of granite and force', 'of substantial size and genuine distinction' (Louis Shaeffer, *Brooklyn Eagle*, 23 Jan. 1953). Yet its notices lacked the wild enthusiasm that had greeted *Death of a Salesman* four years earlier. Whether the reason was discomfort at its political aspects or whether its theatrical climaxes suggested 'mere' melodrama instead of tragedy (as if such climaxes were easy to write or direct), in Broadway terms the implication was a falling-off of dramatic ability.

Reviewers of the first English production in 1954 admired its theatricality. Two years later, critics again responded to its power; by then, it seemed more impressive than before. As Kenneth Tynan put it, its emotional power gained while its political pertinence to McCarthyism receded, and it impressed 'not as an anti-McCarthyite tract but as a devouring study in mass hysteria' (*Observer*, 15 April 1956). By 1965, on the occasion of its next important London production, several reviewers noted the disappearance of its impact as a political parable, though they disagreed where its impact lay, whether 'as an historical melodrama – powerful but crude, sensational and static, rhetorical without being poetic' (Alan Brien, *Sunday Telegraph*, 24 Jan. 1965), in its all-conquering prose that was 'a theatrical weapon as hard and black as iron' (Penelope Gilliatt, *Observer*, 24 Jan. 1965), or in its three-dimensional characters (Martin Esslin, *Plays and Players*, March 1965). Its next major production in America was 1972. While the critics still differed as to whether to call the play a tragedy, Julius Novick spoke for many when he declared (*Village Voice*, 4 May 1972) that

> for all its weaknesses this is a play of size and strength and quality. Miller was wise enough not to push his contemporary implications too far, and so, although Senator Joe McCarthy is many years dead, *The Crucible* has not dated. Its picture of paranoia, raging through society like a plague, is still clear and horribly convincing, still a cogent warning. And *The Crucible* has one old-fashioned virtue that outweighs all its old-fashioned faults: a kind of full-throated, all-out intensity that is very rare in the modern theatre.

By 1980, when Bill Bryden revived it in London, one critic declared unequivocally, 'Time has freed Miller's play from the immediate political situation that inspired it'. It has become 'a rending exploration of a community possessed by the demons of superstition, malice and fear' (David Scott Kastan, *Times Literary Supplement*, 7 Nov. 1980). Another called it 'certainly the best [play] Arthur Miller wrote, possibly the best American play of this century' (B. A. Young, *Financial Times*, 31 Oct. 1980). With each revival, the play's reputation has grown.

18   DIRECTION

Despite the author's care in alternating scenes of theatrical excitement with quiet scenes (Proctor and Abigail alone in Act i, for example, between scenes of threats and hysteria), a frequent dissatisfaction with productions is unrelieved tension that after a while turns tedious. American reviewers lamented that Jed Harris, director of the first production, 'begins the performance at a high pitch of terror and suspicion', which except for two scenes 'he keeps . . . raging to the end' (Brooks Atkinson, *New York Times*, 1 Feb. 1953). Their transatlantic colleagues complained that the first English production, directed by Warren Jenkins, 'is pitched high from the start, and the hysteria is sustained throughout beyond all reasonable expectations' (J. B. Boothroyd, *Punch*, 17 Nov. 1954). 'With playing pitched high almost from the start', came reports of the 1972 revival, 'it was impossible to be moved or even involved in the story' (Douglas Watt, *Daily News*, 28 April 1972).

In America, unless a play has clearly identified American accents, actors usually make no attempt to find American equivalents or to anglicise names. If they act a French play set in France, with people of varied social classes, the American tradition is not to use accents that are Stateside equivalents but to employ general American diction, and Henri does not become Henry. In England, the tradition is different. Attempts are made to find equivalent English dialects and names are often anglicised. With Miller's invented idiom in *The Crucible*, American actors (in every production I have seen, in and outside New York) use general American speech, somewhat modified by the play's distinctive syntax. Not so, English actors. Although one review praised Laurence Olivier's production for dispensing with American accents in favour of 'flat country accents with no particular regional associations' (B. A. Young, *Financial Times*, 20 Jan. 1965), Olivier actually had his actors speak in 'early Cromwellian English', which he admits was 'only a director's guess' (*Confessions of an Actor*, 1982, p. 294). One reviewer confessed himself 'thrown by the assorted accents' in Bill Bryden's production, 'none of them from Massachusetts' (B. A. Young, *Financial Times*, 31 Oct. 1980). Others variously identified them as Irish, a variety of Celtic and rural and robust Warwickshire.

The text offers several opportunities for comedy. Martin Esslin praises Frank Finlay's Giles Corey in Olivier's production for providing 'comic relief' so subtly and with such human wrath that he is able to slide into high tragedy without the slightest jolt' (*Plays and Players*, March 1965). Jed Harris relieved the tension of the original production with some very funny moments. When Proctor gives Danforth Mary's deposition, Hathorn rises and joins him. Parris does the same. After a glance at Proctor, Danforth reads, as do the others, beside him or over his shoulder (Fred Stewart's Parris was a fearful hanger-on who stood on tiptoe to read). Hale, curious as well, joins the group of readers. After a long while, as the nonreaders wait, Danforth stops reading, takes out a handkerchief, and blows his nose – comically capping the silence. But once Walter Hampden (Danforth) left the group, the comedy abruptly stopped. Apparently, Bill Bryden overdid the comedy in this sequence: 'The piece of comic business worked out between the clergyman (Dave Hill) and the deputy governor (Tony Haygarth) where the former keeps leaning on the latter's shoulder in court, seemed to come from a quite different sort of drama' (James Fenton, *Sunday Times*, 2 Nov. 1980).

Critics commented on the force and intensity of Harris's production, which generated a great deal of theatrical excitement. Unfortunately, it seems to have had 'too much excitement and not enough emotion' (Brooks Atkinson, *New York Times*, 23 Jan. 1953), and its vigour was conventional (*Time*, 2 Feb. 1953). As Neil Carson notes, Harris 'lacked Kazan's flair for drawing hidden resources from his actors'. He relied on such big moments as the trial scene, which were among the production's 'chilling, blood-curdling, terrifying' highlights (John Chapman, *Daily News*, 23 Jan. 1953). Missing what John Gassner calls 'the movement toward tragedy', the Proctors' growth in stature was less clear in his staging than in the text (in Ferres). When Miller redirected the play, the production 'acquired a certain human warmth that it lacked amid the shrill excitements of the original version. The hearts of the characters are now closer to the surface than their nerves' (Brooks Atkinson, *New York Times*, 2 July 1953).

While a high-pitched excitement, augmented by sonorous drum rolls for overture and interval, characterised the 1954 production, attention to characterisation was the focus of the English Stage Company production which, thanks to hindsight, now seems to have used the play as practice for its epoch-making production of John Osborne's *Look Back in Anger*, which opened on 8 May 1955, one month less one day after the first performance of *The Crucible*. Directed by Tony Richardson, who with George Devine directed *The Crucible*, the entire cast of *Look Back in Anger* was in the company of Miller's play (including Alan Bates in a bit role sometimes omitted from cast lists).

When Olivier directed *The Crucible* nine years later, he did not overlook the 'massive emotional outbursts' (*Times*, 20 Jan. 1965) or the contrasts of 'teeth-clenching drama and ominous calm' (Bernard Levin, *Daily Mail*, 20 Jan. 1965), but he emphasised the performers, which Jeremy Kingston called 'the best ensemble acting to be seen in London at the present time' (*Punch*, 27 Jan. 1965). In a tribute to this production, Martin Esslin elaborates on this subject (*Plays and Players*, March 1965)

> Spoken without much conviction in the false, histrionic tones some actors will be tempted to adopt, the lines of Miller's last scene must appear as cheap melodrama. It is here that the present production triumphantly demonstrates the value of genuine ensemble acting: the degree of reality that is established is so high that the documentary content of the play, its genuineness as a presentation of events that have really happened, comes across with overwhelming impact.

While Bill Bryden's 1980 production 'makes the most of the succession of climaxes that follow one another with increasing force' (B. A. Young, *Financial Times*, 31 Oct. 1980), they become 'much more moving and memorable' because he presents them 'with no gloating sensationalism' and at the end of the performance 'one is hardly aware that one has been almost $3\frac{1}{2}$ hours in the theatre' (Francis King, *Sunday Telegraph*, 2 Nov. 1980). The company is 'superbly equipped to show the human reality under the still formalities of speech and costume'. After Mark McManus (Proctor) first appears 'as a dour employer, hat pulled straight down over his eyes, threatening his truant servant with the whip', he soon is 'half-capitulating' to Abigail when they are alone together. 'The sense of an austere, frugal existence, in double discipline to the soil and to clerical authority, is inherent in the whole stage picture' (Irving Wardle, *Times*, 5 March 1981). By giving all members of the large cast their moments to reveal themselves, even at the expense of slowing the pace, the result is that the play 'emerges as something more than the drama of one brave man against the crowd. John Proctor . . . is *of* the crowd, as much concerned as they with personal righteousness' (Robert Cushman, *Observer*, 1 Nov. 1980).

As mentioned in the Text section, some critics condemn the play as failed tragedy because while the hero has weaknesses he has no real faults. His seduction of a teenage girl half his age appears not to have impressed them as a major fault. In many productions, this view has an understandable basis. Certainly the girls in the original, though pretty, looked older than teenage; the same was true in the Lincoln Center and Olivier productions. All seemed to be what they actually were, actresses in their twenties. By an ingenious yet (now that he has done it) obvious solution, Bryden intensified the dreadfulness of Proctor's deed in the audience's eyes by casting girls who looked even younger than the seventeen years specified by Miller. Another result, noted Jack Tinker (*Daily Mail*, 6 March 1981), 'The scent of simmering sexual frustration hangs in the air as a girlish fantasy escalates into the hysteria of mass execution'.

Many strikingly realistic details contribute to the effectiveness of Bryden's production. Kastan records that when Abigail 'screams chillingly, claiming to see a yellow bird menacing her, more than one member of the audience . . . turned to see where she pointed. When evil is felt so immediately, we cannot feel easily superior to characters who fall under its sway'. As John and Elizabeth part at the end of Act II, notes Irving Wardle, 'they merely pat each other; full embrace is reserved for the moment before the gallows' (*Times*, 5 March 1981). Each time he sees a production of this play, says Michael Billington, he discovers a new aspect. This time, 'it is the play's powerful evocation of a community in which people are driven to betray friends, neighbours, employers by the pressure of the time. . . . But the real terror is that a man can indict a colleague while still calling him by his Christian name'; and Trevor Ray (Cheever) condemns Proctor 'in a tone of injured comradeship that chills the blood' (*Guardian*, 5 March 1981).

19 SCENERY AND LIGHTING

Miller describes the private rooms that are the settings of the
first two acts as furnished in a spartan manner beneath
exposed roof rafters. A bed is the major furnishing of the first,
establishing illness (that will spread); a pot hanging above a
fire and a table set for dining the second, establishing a family
(that will be imperilled). The public rooms of the last two
acts similarly contrast with each other. The first, used by the
court, has three doors, suggesting the possibility of exit as well
as entry; the second, a prison cell, has only one *'great, heavy
door'*, whose connotations are clear cut.

Dennis Welland has commented appositely on the lighting.
In Act I, the morning sunlight streams through the panes of
a narrow window; in III, sunlight pours through two high
windows; in IV, moonlight seeps through the bars of a high
window. Thus, 'Miller sees the mood of the play – darkness
and gloom penetrated by the single shaft of light cast by
conscientiously dogged goodness'. Unmentioned is the lighting
in Act II. Although stage directions give no explicit indication
at the start of the act, dialogue and directives do so later. 'It's
almost dark', ends Elizabeth's first speech. By the foot of the
next page night has fallen: through the doorway Proctor looks
at the sky, *'absorbing the night'*. The light that enters their home
is extinguished well before the representatives of the life-
extinguishing court arrive.

Perhaps the chief difficulty in designing sets and lighting
for *The Crucible* is to avoid picturesqueness, which tends to
destroy the play's atmosphere. Jo Mielziner, who designed
both for the Lincoln Center production, failed to overcome
this difficulty, and the decorative, prettified scenery (such as
a barred window unit with a lovely blue light behind it in the
last scene) conveyed nothing of the play's world. As John
Simon wrote, 'his lighting at the end fails to evoke the
inexorable approach of a terrible dawn' (*New York*, 15 May
1972).

For the first production, Boris Aronson's unpainted, wide
pine colonial sets conveyed, as several critics noted, a stark,
austere and ominous mood. Six months later, Miller replaced

them with black velour curtains that framed a cyclorama, which light flooded. As *Variety* commented (1 July 1953), 'Lines and action stand out more starkly against the plain cyclorama, the total effect being less realistic, more heightened'.

Apparently more emotionally atmospheric was Patrick Robertson's 'thunder-skied, gibbet-haunted setting' for the Bristol Old Vic (Audrey Williamson, *Contemporary Theatre: 1953–1956*, 1956, p. 183). Motley's design for the English Stage Company employed a tilted wooden frame hung on wires, with minimal peasant furniture on what looked like a hospital-white stage. Also stylised was Hayden Griffin's spare pinewood setting for Bill Bryden's production, with a large wooden shutter revolving and standing or slanting to suggest Parris's loft, Proctor's low-ceilinged room, the meeting house and the cell.

For its three-month tour in 1984, the Royal Shakespeare Company, departing from tradition, used a non-setting. Basically, Bob Crowley created a traverse set that could fit into any venue, including one with catwalks (also used as a playing area) – often a church (such as Christ Church, Spitalfields, and Lincoln Cathedral) or sports hall, with the audience draped around or perched above it, the arrangement also aimed at fitting *The Winter's Tale*, with which *The Crucible* alternated in repertory. As Eric Shorter said, 'the fascination of each show . . . is the circumstance of its staging rather than its performance or interpretation' (*Daily Telegraph*, 22 Oct. 1984). Although some reviewers admired the involvement that derived from the proximity between performers and spectators, more considered the staging inventiveness to be a distraction. When one produces a realistic play, particularly when the acting is realistic, then as Robin Thornber states (*Guardian*, 3 Sept. 1984):

> you break the conventions of naturalism at your peril and not, I think, without good reason. So the microphone used in the court hearing jars. . . . If the officers of the court use electric torches, why don't they drive a car rather than a wooden wagon? And if the floor is carpeted with the oriental rugs from *The Winter's Tale*, scattering straw on it is just plain silly. Shining the follow-spots in the audience's eyes simply breaks the spell.

20 ACTING

John Proctor   Whatever reservations reviewers expressed about
the play or its direction in 1953, they revealed none about
Arthur Kennedy as Proctor. Paying tribute to his moving
honesty as an actor, his sincerity and conviction and the
intellectual clarity he gave the character's motives and feelings,
they felt, as Louis Shaffer stated, that his 'quiet, unforced
strength has never been seen to better advantage' (*Brooklyn
Eagle*, 23 Jan. 1953). These characteristics of his performance
augmented qualities of his persona, including what Seymour
Peck called 'the quality of human frailty'. Kennedy's 'lean,
restless figure, the worried frown on his face, the tense look
in his eyes, always alert to some nameless disaster', were
appropriate to the character of John Proctor. In previous
roles, including Miller's *All My Sons* and *Death of a Salesman*,
Kennedy had played a lost, bewildered young man whose
father was the play's moving force. By contrast, he was the
head of a household in *The Crucible*, and the protagonist as
well. As Peck notes, 'this transformation from the boy of the
earlier plays to the man of *The Crucible*' was a difficult
undertaking, the breaking of a mould. To help the actor
accomplish it, Jed Harris had him dye his hair from its natural
blond to a sombre dark brown. The reason was not to make
the audience look upon him as a different person (after all,
not every spectator would have seen him before) but to make
Kennedy regard himself differently. So he did, and when he
entered, he appeared older and more authoritative (*New York
Times*, 15 Feb. 1953).

The realism of Kennedy's performance contrasts with the
superficial acting of Robert Foxworth at Lincoln Center –
though responsibility may lie with the director, John Berry,
whose lacklustre work helped none of the actors. When Proctor
enters at the start of Act II, Foxworth merely strode onto the
stage, a handsome leading man, as if he had come from
nowhere in particular to nowhere in particular. When Kennedy entered, he had clearly spent a long, hard day planting
in the fields. Kennedy's exhaustion was immediately apparent
(a condition that this Actor's Studio performer was certain to

have worked on). His statement that the farm is a continent when one drops seeds in it foot by foot confirms the impression he gave when he came into the room.

Colin Blakely's performance in Olivier's production seems to have had the same type of credibility. Esslin's description of Blakely (*Plays and Players*, March 1965) actually suggests the performance I saw Kennedy give. First, Esslin contrasts Blakely with an unnamed actor:

> I remember the John Proctor of a performance I saw more than ten years ago (not in this country) emerging from the dungeon where he had been chained up in solidary confinement for months, well scrubbed and neatly made up and delivering his refusal to sign his confession with the tremolo of a Victorian Lear. No wonder one could not believe a word he said. Colin Blakely stumbles on to the stage begrimed and broken, blinded by the light, battered and bruised, reduced almost to a beast, unable to speak, let alone to think. His animal anxiety to save his skin is fully understandable under these circumstances.

In contrast to the former actor, Blakely and Kennedy found the basis of their performance in Miller's stage directions: '*His wrists are chained. He is another man, bearded, filthy, his eyes misty as though webs had overgrown them. He halts inside the doorway, his eye caught by the sight of Elizabeth*'. But notice the difference between the suggestions for the actor and what the actor did. It was Blakely, no doubt aided by Olivier, who stumbled, appeared to be a broken man, was blinded by light, seemed like an animal and had difficulty speaking. The author's words were the start of and inspiration for the actor's creativity. Penelope Gilliatt mentions another of Blakely's feats, one I do not recall in Kennedy's performance: 'In the wild end of Act Three self-loathing burgeons into an avid certainty of sin, and the man of rectitude is not much separated in extremism from the men of law' (*Observer*, 24 Jan. 1965).

In Bill Bryden's production, Mark McManus embodied 'a guilt-racked, God-fearing farmer who looks as if he has sprung from the soil' (Michael Billington, *Guardian*, 5 March 1981). In his Act II scene with his wife, McManus writhed under his mistrustful wife's gaze, 'alternately gentle and lashing out like a staked bull' (Irving Wardle, *Times*, 5 March 1981). His performance 'speaks volumes of fleshy weakness' (Jack

Tinker, *Daily Mail*, 6 March 1981). Maintaining the proper moral balance, he 'goes to his death not as a saint but as a man, aware of his weakness but also of a core of decency and dignity that must not be extinguished' (David Scott Kastan, *Times Literary Supplement*, 7 Nov. 1980).

Elizabeth Proctor Rightly, reviewers praised Beatrice Straight's Elizabeth Proctor in 1953. Whitney Bolton called her 'reserved and cool of exterior, boiling and seething of interior' (*Morning Telegraph*, 24 Jan. 1953), but instead of telegraphing the latter qualities, Straight achieved the more difficult feat of permitting them to emerge. When arrested, Elizabeth says, '*with great fear*: I will fear nothing'. Straight willed herself to overcome her fear before speaking; and when she directed her husband to tell their children she has gone to visit someone who is sick, she betrayed no trepidation but did what Miller describes: looked about the room, trying to fix it in her mind. Her Elizabeth compounded detachment, strength, composure and forceful resolution.

The Lincoln Center production offers a contrast. With slow speech and a trite vocal tremor, Martha Henry played an abstract conception of nobility. When Proctor goes to his death, she imitated the famous 'silent scream' of Helene Weigel, which by 1972 was a cliché (in Bertolt Brecht's *Mother Courage and Her Children*, hostile soldiers bring one of her dead sons to her for identification; aiming to avoid revealing she knows him, she denies the fact, and though her facial muscles move as if she were screaming in pain, no sound emerges).

Like Straight, Joyce Redman played Elizabeth (in the Olivier production) with utter conviction – as one reviewer put it, 'with a painful but masterly reticence' (Harold Hobson, *Sunday Times*, 24 Jan. 1965). As another said, 'Her transformation, from frigidity to moral fulfilment, is one of the beauties of the production' (*Times*, 20 Jan. 1965). Particularly impressive was the ensemble work in her scenes with Colin Blakely, which Penelope Gilliatt called 'low-toned marvels of intimacy' (*Observer*, 24 Jan. 1965). In their first scene together, 'Miss Redman reproachfully unforthcoming, Mr. Blakely embarrassed and uneasy', their dialogue was 'quietly spoken and spread with silences' – in striking contrast to the shrieks of the possessed girls that concluded the previous scene (Jeremy Kingston, *Punch*, 27 Jan. 1965).

When Bill Bryden's National Theatre production transferred to the West End, Lynn Farleigh assumed the role of Elizabeth. Beginning by 'conveying a permanent sense of accusation through her gauntly handsome presence' (Michael Billington, *Guardian*, 5 March 1981), she 'proceeds to a wonderful expression of extreme emotions with the minimum of physical means' (Irving Wardle, *Times*, 5 March 1981).

Reverend John Hale   As John McClain said of the original production, E. G. Marshall brought 'warmth and sympathy' to the role of Hale (*New York Journal American*, 23 Jan. 1953). A bright-eyed, eager young man filled with love of the work for which he has prepared himself, he personified Miller's description of one who 'conceives of himself much as a young doctor on his first call'. He aimed to spread the light of scientific knowledge on the darkness of ignorant superstition, never dreaming in his naiveté that his knowledge was pseudo-knowledge. When Marshall spoke of his disillusionment in Act IV – he arrived in Salem like a bridegroom happily greeting his bride with confidence and religious fervour, but what he touched died – he seemed not only to describe the way he played the role in Act I, but also to feel betrayed by what he held most dearly.

In the Olivier production, Robert Lang made a transition 'from soft-voiced fanaticism to disillusioned frenzy' (*Times*, 20 Jan. 1965). In Bryden's staging, James Grant was 'intensely chilling' in Acts I and II, 'as his murderous arguments are coming from palpably the most rational and gentle-natured figure on stage' (Irving Wardle, *Times*, 31 Oct. 1980). By contrast, Philip Bosco, at Lincoln Center, failed to suggest Hale's essential integrity and, perhaps prompted by the director, tried to convey Hale's inner turmoil by vocal tension and 'indicating' (i.e. superficially making a dramatic point of an emotion, without inner conviction).

Abigail Williams The eyes of Madeleine Sherwood, who played Abigail in 1953, glowed with lust in Act I. In Act III they gleamed with a kind of mad craftiness. Perhaps the most impressive Abigail has been that of Sarah Miles in 1965. A 'plaguingly sexy mixture of beauty and crossness' (Penelope Gilliatt, *Observer*, 24 Jan. 1965), Miles 'reeks with the cunning of suppressed evil and steams with the promise of suppressed passion' (Milton Shulman, *Evening Standard*, 20 Jan. 1965). Malcolm Rutherford describes her 'tremendous performance' in vivid detail:

> Abigail does not have much to say. For much of the time she is not even on the stage. She is a presence and Miss Miles establishes her at once. She seems to play the part almost entirely with her body. Very early in the play and at a time when he has little cause to suspect her the Reverend Parris asks her of her part in the proceedings in the forest. One notices the coyness, the blushing, the suspicious look in her eyes far more than her actual reply. When she is finally challenged in the courtroom one is struck not by her stammering replies but by the way her hair suddenly loosens and falls about her face in confusion.

In this courtroom, Proctor, ashamed of his sexual activities with her and accusing her of intending to murder his wife, barely looks at her. But Miles's 'longing eyes are on Proctor all the time. She receives almost no recognition. It is a brilliant, even a solo performance' (*Spectator*, 29 Jan. 1965). How does another actress follow such a performance? In Bill Bryden's production, Carolyn Embling went in a different direction. Instead of embodying a 'star temptress', she performed 'a commonplace girl, thus reducing Proctor's "lechery" to truthful domestic proportions' (Irving Wardle, *Times*, 31 Oct. 1980). Let us recall that this is the production in which the accusing girls appeared to be young teenagers, not (like Sherwood and Miles) women in their twenties.

Deputy Governor, Judge Danforth On several occasions, Arthur Miller has expressed regret that he did not make Danforth, the chief judge, as thoroughly evil as he was in real life. Happily, the dramatist did not express his second thoughts in revisions. As written, Danforth has numerous facets and different aspects of his character. At Lincoln Center, Stephen Elliott may have taken his cue from Miller's statements about Danforth, for the actor snarled through the production as an outright villain. In the Bryden production, Tony Haygarth showed him to be 'a man of fierce blinkered integrity' (Michael Billington, *Guardian*, 5 March 1981). At the Bristol Old Vic, John Kidd presented him as 'a man honestly desiring to do right and to seek justice', a person 'with pedantic integrity', 'genuinely concerned to see justice done' (Harold Hobson, *Sunday Times*, 14 Nov. 1954). At the Royal Court, George Devine played the judge 'not as a man of fine legal integrity but as a man with a good share of the credulity and intolerance that has swept Salem' (*Times*, 10 April 1956). In Olivier's production, Anthony Nicholls performed 'the upright judge' with 'dignity, majesty and implacable wrong-headedness' (Bernard Levin, *Daily Mail*, 20 Jan. 1965).

Probably the most impressive Danforth was the first, Walter Hampden, in 1953 a grand old man of the New York stage. Almost 74 years of age, he carried with him the impressiveness of a lifetime of splendid work in the theatre, a career that had begun in 1901. Such terms as authority and dignity frequently appear in reviews of his performance. Hampden's Danforth 'rules over the court proceedings with a terrible patriarchial mien' (John Beaufort, *Christian Science Monitor*, 31 Jan. 1953), which was 'bland, icy and relentless' (John Chapman, *Daily News*, 23 Jan. 1953). He 'truly believes what he is doing and can never doubt the accusers' (George Freedley, *Morning Telegraph*, 7 Feb. 1953). His performance transmitted 'implacable righteousness' (Brooks Atkinson, *New York Times*, 2 July 1953) and 'a towering fanaticism that is enormously effective since it conveys the vengeful self-righteousness of the true theocrat' (Brooks Atkinson, *New York Times*, 1 Feb. 1953).

Reverend Samuel Parris   In the original production, Fred Stewart acted Parris as a weasel of a man – partly servile, fearful and fawning; partly angry as one so often thwarted can be angry, venting his frustrations on social inferiors. In the opening scene, his hands clasped in prayer, he tearfully and fervently prayed for his daughter; he almost snarled when he commanded Tituba, who was wholly at his mercy; later, he grovelled and slavered as he failed to conceal his obsequiousness before Danforth, particularly when it seemed the judge might turn his sympathies in a different direction.

According to Martin Esslin, Kenneth Mackintosh, who acted Parris in 1965, revealed 'a depth of background that makes one sorry for the poor man, so insecure that he *must* go to any length to make a success of his last professional chance' (*Plays and Players*, March 1965). In 1980, Tony Hill played him as a 'panic-stricken' and 'job-conscious' man. 'His blanched, terrified face is the first promise of the calamitous division of the community into the falsely accused, and their revengeful, and envious accusers' (Irving Wardle, *Times*, 31 Oct. 1980).

Mary Warren   Whereas Fred Stewart as Parris suggested a weasel, Jennie Egan, who played Mary in 1953, suggested a mouse; and one may infer that both, trained in the 'method' school of American acting, employed animal imagery in their preparation of the roles. Warrant for Egan's mouselike characterisation comes from the dialogue: Proctor refers to her as a mouse; and while Elizabeth claims Mary is no longer a mouse, subsequent events prove her wrong. As played by Egan, Mary's eyes darted fearfully from one adult to another, as if each were a large animal capable of devouring her. Her whimpering repetitions of 'I cannot' at the end of Act II demonstrated the shaky grounds on which Proctor would base his case. In the Olivier production, Jeanne Hepple was 'wonderfully pop-eyed in her distraction' (Philip Hope-Wallace, *Guardian*, 20 Jan. 1965). In Bryden's version, Valerie Whittington veered 'frighteningly between little-girl innocence and experienced wickedness' (B. A. Young, *Financial Times*, 31 Oct. 1980).

READING LIST

Quotations and paraphrases of the plays are from the texts in Arthur Miller, *Collected Plays* (1960). Unless otherwise indicated, Miller's comments are identified by the title of the essay and are in *The Theatre Essays of Arthur Miller* (1978). Excerpts from Elia Kazan's notebook and annotated script are in Kenneth Thorpe Rowe, *A Theatre in Your Head* (1960). Jo Mielziner's *Designing for the Theatre* (1965) contains his records.

Particularly valuable to the study of these plays are collections of important essays, cited alphabetically by the surname of the editors: Robert A. Corrigan, *Arthur Miller: A Collection of Critical Essays* (1969); John H. Ferres, *Twentieth Century Interpretations of The Crucible* (1972); John D. Hurrell, *Two Modern American Tragedies: Reviews and Criticisms of Death of a Salesman and A Streetcar Named Desire* (1961); Robert A. Martin, *Arthur Miller: New Perspectives* (1962); James J. Martine, *Critical Essays on Arthur Miller* (1979); Walter J. Meserve *The Merrill Studies in Death of a Salesman* (1972); Gerald Weales, *The Crucible: Text and Criticism* (1971) and *Death of a Salesman: Text and Criticism* (1967).

Among book-length studies by individual authors, the following works are informative and useful: Neil Carson, *Arthur Miller* (1982); Ronald Hayman, *Arthur Miller* (1972); Edward Murray, *Arthur Miller* (1967); Benjamin Nelson, *Arthur Miller: Portrait of a Playwright* (1970); Dennis Welland, *Miller the Playwright* (1983).

Helpful books about tragedy and collections with essays on tragedy are: Normand Berlin, *The Secret Cause* (1961); Robert W. Corrigan (ed.), *Tragedy: Vision and Form* (1965); Bernard F. Dukore (ed.), *Dramatic Theory and Criticism* (1974); Robert B. Heilman, *Tragedy and Melodrama* (1968); Clifford Leech, *Tragedy* (1969); Vladimir Nabokov, 'The Tragedy of Tragedy', in *The Man from the USSR and Other Plays with two essays on the drama* (1985); Elder Olson, *Tragedy and the Theory of Drama* (1986); John Orr, *Tragic Drama and Modern Society* (1981); D. D. Raphael, *The Paradox of Tragedy* (1961); George Steiner, *The Death of Tragedy* (1963); Raymond Williams, *Modern Tragedy* (1967).

Other works, which contain useful material, include: C. W. E. Bigsby, *A Critical Introduction to Twentieth-Century American Drama*, vol. 2 (1984); Enoch Brater, 'Ethics and Ethnicity in the Plays of Arthur Miller', in *From Hester Street to Hollywood*, ed. S. B. Cohen (1983); Richard I. Evans, *Psychology and Arthur Miller* (1969); John Gassner, *The Theatre in Our Times* (1954); Arthur Miller, *Salesman in Beijing* (1984); Thomas E. Porter, *Myth and Modern American Drama* (1969).

INDEX OF NAMES